THE MYSTERY OF CHRIST

To Rebecca!
For the story of
God, Christ is in us!

Shay

THE MYSTERY OF CHRIST:
A RADICAL TRUTH...LIVED

SHAY A. MECKENSTOCK

a limited liability company
Hays, Kansas

The Mystery of Christ: A Radical Truth...Lived

Cover Design by Mathias Clay Leeson
Interior Design by Gennifer A. Marconette
Edited by Gennifer A. Marconette

AURA PRODUCTIONS LLC
106 West 17th, Hays, KS 67601
www.auraproductions.org

Library of Congress Cataloging-in-Publication Data

Meckenstock, Shay A.
      The mystery of Christ : a radical truth-- lived /
Shay A. Meckenstock.
      p. cm.
      Includes bibliographical references.
      LCCN 2007925462
      ISBN-13: 978-0-9794167-0-5
      ISBN-10: 0-9794167-0-1

      1. Christian life. 2. Jesus Christ--Kingdom.
I. Title.

BV4501.3.M43 2007   248.4
                      QBI07-600171

Printed in the United States by Morris Publishing
3212 East Highway 30
Kearney, NE 68847
1-800-650-7888

To the Family Church of Hays,
Thank you for pressing in with me to discover the truths that set us free. Without you, none of this would be possible.

ACKNOWLEDGMENTS

Special thanks to Karen Rigler for writing the study guide that accompanies each chapter.

To Matt Bennett for suggesting the study guide as a benefit to the book.

To Mathias Clay Leeson for his creativity in designing the cover.

To Gennifer Marconette for looking after all the publishing details and getting this book to print.

And finally, a big thanks to my husband, Bobb, who has always been my greatest supporter and the love of my life.

"Historic Christianity, biblical Christianity, believes that Christianity is not just doctrinal truth, but flaming truth...a truth that can be verbalized and then lived."

Francis Schaeffer
The Great Evangelical Disaster

PREFACE

A RADICAL TRUTH...LIVED

Jesus counseled the latter day Church to buy gold, white garments, and eye salve.[1] The gold is for faith, the white garments are for righteousness, and the eye salve is for vision. I discovered that faith without righteousness will not get one very far, but a defect in spiritual vision will lead one down the wrong road to begin with.

The Church today needs all three—faith, righteousness, vision—but must begin with a correction in spiritual vision. And just as Jesus in His time spoke truth about Who He was, but the revelation of that truth came by way of the Holy Spirit, so it is in this day. The Word speaks the truth and the Holy Spirit brings the light of the revelation upon the Word.

There is a church emerging in these last days all over the world that lives a radical truth. I know because I see it emerging around me in a generation of 20-somethings. This first book is not so much about their journey as much as it is about the radical message that Jesus proclaimed in His gospel of the kingdom of God, and the demand it makes for a decision that causes a change in spiritual vision that transforms lives today like it did 2,000 years ago.

IT BEGINS AT THE BOTTOM

I do not believe the current Church is undergoing revival or reformation, but is instead being radically revolutionized. I am not the first to voice this opinion, but I may be the first to say it is not being revolutionized from the top down, but from the bottom up. I say this for two reasons.

(1) The bottom is where the foundation is.
(2) The bottom is where all those whose lives are shattered, broken, and in bondage sit and wait for the church to provide real answers for life's real problems.

In regards to the first, unless the foundation of the church changes, all we will have is the current model of church with new titles and re-formed programs. This is already happening. Regarding the second, people are getting tired of waiting, and the problems of life are getting more difficult and oppressive. Is anyone listening to their cries?

I hear the same message today that Paul had for Timothy:[2]

For God has not given us a spirit of fear, but of power and of love and of a sound mind. Therefore do not be ashamed of the testimony of the Lord, nor of me His prisoner, but share with me in the sufferings for the gospel according to the power of God, who has saved us and called us with a holy calling, not according to our works, but according to His own purpose and grace which was given to us in Christ Jesus before time began, but has now been revealed by the appearing of our Savior Jesus Christ, who has abolished death and brought life and immortality to light through the gospel.

The gospel according to the power of God. A holy calling according to God's own purpose and grace, founded in Christ before time began.

Why is there a need for starting with the correct vision? Or right message? Because what you see and hear is what you pursue. If you see and hear a message that God loves you, saves you, and wants to bless you, then that is what you will pursue— His blessings. You will see and hear that Jesus sits at the right hand of the Father, interceding on your behalf, to obtain the things you are needing or longing for. This is where we got it all wrong.

Jesus sits at the right hand of the Father interceding on our behalf for the purpose of the Father, not for the purpose of man.[3]

So what of the Father? The Bible speaks of His inheritance in the saints. What, then, is God's inheritance in us? The riches of the glory of His inheritance in the saints.[4] What, then, is the Father's will?

Paul says it is a mystery—a secret—hidden from generations, but now revealed. The generations past heard of the prophecies regarding the Messiah, the Christ. So what was hidden from them that the Church is to proclaim to the world, and even make known to the principalities and powers in heavenly places today?

This is the radical truth—God's secret—that is to be lived. Not just known, but lived!

It is a truth greater than the Messiah has come, His name is Jesus the Christ, and He saves as well as heals and delivers. This message was not a mystery to the early church, for it had been prophesied. So, too, had the kingdom of God. "In the days of these kings the God of heaven will set up a kingdom which shall never be destroyed."[5]

What is God's mystery that Paul was called to preach and teach, not in word only but in the power of the Holy Spirit? Therein lies a clue—the Holy Spirit.

What we are talking about is a Spirit-revealed gospel of the living Truth.

If you see and hear a man-centered gospel, then that is what you will live out.

If you see and hear a God-centered gospel, His eternal purpose, this again, is what you will live out.

The radical truth is about a God-centered gospel, His eternal purpose, as revealed by the Holy Spirit even today.

My prayer for this book is that it might be the salve for the eyes of the body of Christ so that she may see again that which God purchased for Himself with the blood of His own Son. It is not what He bought for us. It is what He bought back for Himself that He now puts in us. To know this truth is radical for today. To live it will require the life of another; and this is the Mystery of Christ.

TABLE OF CONTENTS

"God, who has saved us and called us with
a holy calling, not according to our works,
but according to His own purpose and grace
which was given to us in
Christ Jesus before time began,
but has now been revealed by the appearing of our
Savior Jesus Christ, who has abolished death and
brought life and immortality to light through the gospel."
2 Timothy 1:9-10

INTRODUCTION

The Church today is engaged in a war over reality. What we see and hear in the New Testament scriptures is not what we see and hear in the reality of our lives today as Christians. We could argue whether it should still resemble the New Testament church, but when hurting people are turning away from the church to find answers for life's real problems elsewhere one must begin to ask, "If God is real, then where is He? Where is the glory of God in the church today?'

The gospel message of salvation and eternal security, though true, has not addressed the brokenness and captivity that God's people experience today. About eight years ago, as I studied the scriptures to find God's answers to the cries for help, I noticed two things: first, the gospel message Jesus preached and Paul took to the Gentiles is different than the gospel of salvation we hear in our churches today; second, wherever this gospel of the kingdom of God was preached, healing, deliverance, signs, and miracles followed. In Paul's letter to the Corinthians he wrote:

> And my speech and my preaching were not with persuasive words of human wisdom, but in demonstration of the Spirit and of power, that your faith should not be in the wisdom of men but in the power of God. However, we speak wisdom among those who are mature, yet not the wisdom of this age, nor of the rulers of this age, who are coming to nothing. But we speak the wisdom of God in a mystery, the hidden wisdom which God ordained before the ages for our glory.[1]

What is this hidden wisdom that God ordained before the ages? And how is it designed for our glory? I began to sense that we were missing something that is meant to be vitally important to our life in Christ Jesus.

DIFFERENT GOSPELS

When we turn to the modern church to find answers for our troubled lives, we hear a message that says God loves us and saves us for eternity. Its central premise is that man was created for utopia, the Garden of Eden; man fell out of relationship with God because of sin; yet through the redeeming work of Jesus Christ man is once again able to inherit the eternal security of heaven. But is this the full wisdom of God? Is this His full counsel?

When Paul wrote to Timothy that "[God] saved us and called us with a holy calling, not according to our works, but according to His own purpose and grace which was given to us in Christ Jesus before time began, but has now been revealed by the appearing of our Savior Jesus Christ,"[2] Paul was telling

Timothy (and us) several things:

(1) We are saved and called with a holy calling.
(2) Neither the salvation nor the calling is according to our works, but is according to God's own purpose and grace.
(3) This salvation and grace was given to us in Christ Jesus before time began.

Salvation and the holy calling are two separate things. We know what salvation is, but what is a holy calling? We know that we are saved by grace and not by our works, but what does it mean to be called according to God's own purpose? And why is it important to know that this purpose and grace were given before time began?

I am suggesting that the modern gospel of salvation has reduced the gospel of the kingdom of God in half. We are left holding on to a man-centered gospel, versus the God-centered gospel called the gospel of the kingdom of God.

A HOLY CALLING

A holy calling is more than salvation. Salvation by grace through the death and resurrection of Jesus Christ is what God provides in order that mankind may once again stand in the presence of God as he was in the day Adam was created. But it does not answer the question, "For what purpose did God call man forth after He created him?" God's purpose and destiny for man does not begin in the Garden of Eden with man's fall and subsequent need for salvation. God's purpose and destiny began in the heart of the Godhead before the creation of man. The call of man is to put forth the image and likeness of God upon the earth.

GOD'S PURPOSE

DeVern Fromke wrote in *Ultimate Intention,*

> Perhaps nothing has so blighted the vision and
> growth of believers as the false assumption that
> Adam in his innocence and sinless state was all
> that God ever purposed him to be. It is this error
> which leads many to believe that God's highest
> intention is to restore man's lost paradise. This
> kind of reasoning is the fruit of a wrong starting
> point.[3]

When restoration becomes our end goal, then our needs
become the reason for Jesus' sacrifice. We turn aside from God's
purpose to live ours, with the expectation of His blessing upon
our self-rule. When, in fact, God purposed that man would be
indwelt with his own life—the life of Christ in the Holy Spirit—
and so manifest to the world Himself through us.

THE IMPORTANCE OF TIMING

"Before time began" means the plans and purposes of
God are eternal, fixed and unchangeable as they are outside of
time. Isaiah was told by God to remember the former things of
old, "For I am God, and there is no other; I am God, and there
is none like Me, declaring the end from the beginning, and from
ancient times things that are not yet done, saying, 'My counsel
shall stand, and I will do My pleasure.'"[4]

You may have already noted that I designed this book
in three parts. Each part represents a particular Being of the
Godhead: Father, Son, and Holy Spirit. As I study the scriptures
and listen to the voice of God, I notice again and again how each
One communicated differently to unveil the mystery of Christ

with increasing revelation over the passage of time. The Father wills, the Son speaks and manifests the Word, and the Holy Spirit brings divine revelation. By telling their story separately, I hope to convey to you, the reader, the great depths and purposes of God in order that you may be fully established in them.

At the end of each chapter are study questions to help facilitate your own discovery of truth. God bless you as you endeavor to live out the truths as a community of Saints empowered by the Holy Spirit.

As Paul wrote to the Corinthians, "Eye has not seen, nor ear heard, nor have entered into the heart of man the things which God has prepared for those who love Him. But God has revealed them to us through His Spirit."[5]

So now let us begin, not with creation, the fall, or the dominion of man, but with a discovery of the will of the Father before time began.

PART I

THE WISDOM OF GOD IN A MYSTERY

"But we speak the wisdom of God in a mystery,
the hidden wisdom which God
ordained before the ages for our glory."
1 Corinthians 2:7

Chapter One

BEFORE TIME BEGAN

I have heard it said that timing is everything. Is it not true that if you enter the telling of a story or joke halfway through, then you are more than likely to be the one with the baffled look on your face at the end? You missed something key to the story. Better to have caught it from the beginning.

Well, this is how some Christians are today—baffled. I think it is because they missed the beginning of the story. Following the day of their salvation, they wonder why they don't "feel" any different, or if there is more to this so-called "new life" and they somehow missed it. They came in to the family of God hearing that because of their misbehavior they are in need of saving grace; Jesus Christ is the One who can supply their need, and, as a special gift, grant them a promise of eternal life. To think that God's best is to restore us for paradise leaves a whole lot out of the greater equation called the mystery of Christ. This mystery, the beginning of the story, occurs first in the heart of the Father before the foundation of the world was established. It is a story of a King, called the Son of Man, and His Bride, who together inherit a kingdom. A future glimpse of this King and His Bride is in Matthew 25:31, 34, "When the Son of Man comes in His glory, and all the holy angels with Him…then the King will say to those on His right hand, 'Come, you blessed of My Father, inherit the kingdom prepared for you from the foundation of the world.'"

What is this kingdom and who is the Bride? These are great mysteries left out of our modern evangelistic gospel of salvation by grace, yet they are presented to us in Genesis before Adam and Eve ever sinned. The beginning of the story tells your future, if Christ is found in you. It is a glorious future that is available to live today, not just when you die.

THE BEGINNING OF THE STORY

Before man was created, and Adam and Eve sinned, you were in the mind of Christ. In Scripture, the first mention of man is in Genesis 1:26; God says, "Let *Us* make man in Our image, according to Our likeness; let them have dominion over the fish of the sea, over the birds of the air, and over the cattle, over all the earth and over every creeping thing that creeps on the earth."

When the Godhead—represented by the *Us* in Genesis 1:26—decided to make man, they decided to make him in the image of God. *Image*, meaning to re-present something to someone. *Likeness*, meaning to be similar in nature. The conceptual idea is God wants man to represent Him on earth.

Because God is Spirit, mankind must also be fashioned with a spirit in order to bare forth His likeness. God "formed man of the dust of the ground, and breathed into his nostrils the breath of life; and man became a living soul."[1] Man was created with three parts: It was from the dust that man was given a *body*, from God's own breath that man was given a *spirit*; thus, man became a living *soul*.

It is important to recognize the likeness of man's nature to God's nature: because man and God are both spirit, it is in man's spirit that he is most like God. "...[The Lord] stretches out the heavens, lays the foundation of the earth, and forms the spirit of man within him."[2] It is in man's spirit and God's Spirit where the two meet.

Watchman Nee, writing at the beginning of the last century, wrote in *The Normal Christian Life*:

> What was [God's] purpose? God wanted to have a race...whose members were gifted with a spirit whereby communion would be possible with Himself, who is Spirit. The race, possessing God's own life, was to cooperate in securing His purposed end by defeating every possible uprising of the enemy and undoing his evil works...He is concerned with bringing us into, and bringing into us something Adam never had...It is something positive and purposeful, going far beyond the recovery of a lost position.[3]

MAN PURPOSED TO BE A VESSEL FOR THE DIVINE LIFE

What God first declares by His Word, He later expands with divine revelation from His Holy Spirit. We see this occurring with Paul in his letter to the Ephesians. He accredits the Holy Spirit as being the One who revealed to him the mystery of Christ—that both Gentiles and Jews should be fellow heirs of the same body, and partakers of His promise in Christ through the gospel.[4] Heirs of the same body and partakers of His promise. This begs the question, "Whose body? And what was

His promise?"

We are called to be an inheritor of the very life of God. We are not called to imitate a great Teacher, a kind Person who did wonderful things. No, we are called to inherit and be a vessel that carries His life in us. Not imitation, but inheritance.

We see this first expressed in The Tree of Life when God commanded Adam and Eve to freely eat of every tree of the garden save one.[5] The same life that was in God's breath was in the Tree of Life. The Hebrew word for Life is *chay*[6]. The same word in Greek is *zoë*.[7] John of the gospel said this of Jesus Christ, "In Him was life [zoë], and the life [zoë] was the light of men."[8] As Adam and Eve ate of the Tree of Life, they were partaking of the very life of Jesus Christ. Jesus said this of His own life, "It is the Spirit who gives life [zoë]; the flesh profits nothing. The words that I speak to you are spirit, and they are life [zoë]."[9] Then later, Paul, by revelation of this same Spirit, tells us that whereas the first Adam became a living soul, the last Adam, Jesus, became a life-giving spirit.[10]

PARTAKERS OF HIS PROMISE

The life of Jesus Christ comes in to us through the Holy Spirit, the Spirit of God. Jesus taught the disciples about the Holy Spirit saying, "Behold, I send the Promise of My Father," and so commanded them to "wait for the Promise."[11] Then, after His resurrection, He went to them in the upper room, pronounced peace to them, breathed on them, and said, "Receive the Holy Spirit."[12] Just like He had done once before, a long time ago, to Adam!

Before His crucifixion, Jesus prayed:

Father, the hour has come. Glorify Your Son, that
Your Son also may glorify You, as You have given
Him authority over all flesh, that He should give

eternal life to as many as You have given Him. And this is eternal life, that they may know You, the only true God, and Jesus Christ whom You have sent. I have glorified You on the earth. I have finished the work which You have given Me to do. And now, O Father, glorify Me together with Yourself, with the glory which I had with You before the world was.[13]

The promise had been fulfilled. Having believed, the disciples (as well as you) were sealed with the Holy Spirit of promise.[14] Eternal life is a relationship with God through the body of Jesus Christ. It is not a place: it is a Life. It is a Life that is alive in you, and His name is the Holy Spirit. Our life, abundant and forever, was planned from the beginning to be formed in Christ Jesus. His Spirit in us is Colossians 1:27, "Christ in you, the hope of glory."

THE PERFECT MAN

As Christ is formed in us collectively, we become what the Bible refers to as the one perfect man.[15] Christ and His Body become one. In this way Christ has His preeminence: "for it pleased the Father that in Him all the fullness should dwell, and by Him to reconcile all things to Himself, by Him, whether things on earth or things in heaven, having made peace through the blood of His cross."[16] This is the Spirit of Christ in one believer touching the Spirit of Christ in another believer, which then manifests the Presence of God before the world. It is God's great passion to reveal Himself to the world through human expression. No single individual outside of Jesus Christ could do this, but collectively we can, and this is the glory of God.

THE BRIDE

A more romantic picture of Christ and His Body is called the Bride. The spiritual church—not the religious church—those born of God, born of His Sprit, are betrothed to His Son and called the Bride. She is one with Him because she has been born out of His side. We can see this in the Garden and on the Cross.

Return with me now to the Garden, for it is a "type," or picture, of your destiny. Remember, everything God does is first in the natural, and then brought to a greater light of revelation by the Holy Spirit. God made Adam from the dust of the ground outside of the Garden, but He brought forth Eve from Adams's side rib inside the Garden. At the end of Genesis 2 we read, "Therefore a man shall leave his father and mother and be joined to his wife, and they shall become one flesh." And in Ephesians we read "For we are members of His body, of His flesh and of His bones. 'For this reason a man shall leave his father and mother and be joined to his wife, and the two shall become one flesh.' This is a great mystery, but I speak concerning Christ and the church."[17] Likewise, whereas we are first born physically, outside of heaven, and are earthy, our spirits are born anew of God, out of the pierced side of Jesus as He died on the Cross,[18] and we are now bone of His bone and flesh of His flesh.

This new creation *is* His Bride—the Church—and the one who is seated next to Him in the heavenly places.[19] Today she is a spiritual temple, but in the future she will be a physical city.

THE END IS REVEALED FROM THE BEGINNING

And so it is that the end is revealed from the beginning. From the Garden of Eden we are given a picture of the holy city, New Jerusalem, coming down out of heaven from God, prepared as a bride adorned for her husband. And just as in the Garden of Eden there was a river and the Tree of Life, so shall it be in the end in the new city called the Bride.[20] The river watered the garden in Eden[21] and is called the "water of life" in Revelation 22:1. As the river watered the Tree of Life in the beginning, so it does in the end—proceeding from the throne of God and of the Lamb. Therefore, the Life is in the river.

Jesus said to the woman at the well, "If you knew the gift of God, and who it is who says to you, 'Give me a drink,' you would have asked Him, and He would have given you living water."[22] We call this gift Eternal life. He is the Holy Spirit. The Testaments of God close with these words, "The Spirit and the bride say 'Come!' And let him who hears say, 'Come!' And let him who thirsts come. Whoever desires, let him take the water of life freely."[23]

From the beginning of His story, we discover the calling and destiny of God for our lives. Created in His image and likeness we are to be a temple for the living God;[24] a dwelling place of God in the Spirit[25] in order that, through mankind, God may establish His kingdom on earth as it is in heaven.

There is however, another kingdom that opposes God's kingdom and is at war to destroy God's plans and purposes. Paul himself feared "lest somehow, as the serpent deceived Eve by his craftiness, so your minds may be corrupted from the simplicity that is in Christ."[26] Let us see who the enemy of God is.

STUDY QUESTIONS

1. Is there more to the gospel of the kingdom of God besides forgiveness of sin and a future in heaven? Why do you believe this?

2. How does God communicate with us today? How does thinking of yourself as first and foremost a spirit man influence you?

3. Being an inheritor of the very life of God brings purpose and hope, as opposed to imitating Christ, which adds fuel to the fire of rules, regulations, and religion. Why would God purpose us to inherit versus imitate?

4. What is the definition of eternal life as spoken by the Lord Jesus Christ? How does your perspective change knowing that eternal life begins now?

Chapter Two

TWO KINGDOMS IN CONFLICT

WE WILL NOT FULLY UNDERSTAND GOD'S
WILL FOR US—HIS CHURCH—IF WE DO NOT
UNDERSTAND THE PROBLEM OF EVIL.

Man is God's most glorious creation: part physical, of
the earth, and part spiritual, of the heavens. Indeed, even the
angels are in awe of man; angels were given the assignment to
minister to those who will inherit salvation, for man was created
a 'little lower than God (Elohim), crowned with honor and glory,
and given charge over all the creation.'[1]

There were, however, some angels who were not at all
happy about God's plans for man, for you see, they followed
another host. Long before there was rebellion on earth, there
was a rebellion in heaven.

WAR IN HEAVEN

The rebellion is recorded in Revelation 12:7-9.

And war broke out in heaven: Michael and his angels fought with the dragon; and the dragon and his angels fought, but they did not prevail, nor was a place found for them in heaven any longer. So the great dragon was cast out, that serpent of old, called the Devil and Satan, who deceives the whole world; he was cast to the earth, and his angels were cast out with him.

Earlier, in Revelation 12:4, we read that the number of angels who followed Satan's rebellion was one-third of the angelic host. The exact time of this rebellion is uncertain, but there is a theory, called The Gap theory, that places the rebellion between Genesis 1:1 and Genesis 1:2.

The Bible states in Genesis 1:1, "In the beginning God created the heavens and the earth." And in verse 2 it says, "The earth was without form, and void; and darkness was on the face of the deep. And the Spirit of God was hovering over the face of the waters."

In 1814, a scholar by the name of Thomas Chalmers compared Genesis 1:2 with Isaiah 45:18, which reads, "For thus says the LORD, Who created the heavens, Who is God, Who formed the earth and made it, Who has established it, Who did not create it in vain, Who formed it to be inhabited: I am the LORD, and there is no other."

According to Chalmers, the term "without form and void," *tohu v'bohu*, seems to indicate that the earth was not originally created without form and void but subsequently became that way. In fact, the verb in that sentence translated "was"—*haya*—means "became;" it is a transitive verb implying action. So verse 2 could be translated, 'But the earth became without form and void.' The word for "but" is an adversative in both the Septuagint (ancient Greek translation) and the Vulgate (Latin). One suggestion from this hint in verse 2 is the possibility of a gap—an interval of time (maybe billions of years), between verses 1 and 2. Not all Bible scholars and scientists agree with this theory, but it could be a possible explanation for the age of the earth, which clearly is older than 6,000 or 7,000 years as young earth creationists would have you believe.[2]

Since Satan and his angels were cast down to earth, heaven was no longer his domain; this is why he is called the Prince of this world. The Gap Theory suggests that God judged the earth and it became without form and void: ruined and uninhabitable due to Satan's influence. Verse 2 and forward may describe a re-creation, a reconstruction of the earth. "And the Spirit of God was hovering on the face of the waters"[3]; and rather than wipe out the earth, God chose to undertake a plan of redemption.[4]

INVASION OF THE KINGDOM OF DARKNESS

The Garden of Eden was God's "theatre of operation" for establishing His government on earth as it is in heaven; the Adamic race was His chosen, created vessel. As per his nature, Satan schemes to corrupt the image of God—man—and God's kingdom of Light. He looks for a way in. Because Satan cannot enter man or his world without a legal, open door, he looks for an opportunity to tempt man into violating God's law. If he succeeds, and a violation of the law occurs, he has legal ground on which to enter.

Satan tempts Adam and Eve into questioning God's word by asking them, "Has God indeed said, 'You shall not eat of every tree of the garden'?"[5] Notice the question was misquoted, but the point is that the evil one could even speak. By agreement with Satan they commit a violation of the only law God had given them, "Of every tree of the garden you may freely eat; but of the tree of the knowledge of good and evil you shall not eat..."[6]

THE NATURE OF EVIL

Satan's tactics with Adam and Eve illustrate the nature of evil. Evil comes to us through the thought life of dis-embodied spirits. God Himself points this out to Adam, and to us, in Genesis 3 when God comes to speak to Adam in the cool of the evening, as was His custom. This particular time, however, God cannot find Adam. When God asks him why he is hiding, he replies that he was afraid because he was naked; to which God says, "Who told you that you were naked? Have you eaten from the tree of which I commanded you that you should not eat?"[7] *Who* told you? In other words, a disembodied spirit inhabited the form of a being, either human or animal, both of which angels and disembodied spirits can inhabit and speak through.

Cain's experience also gives us a picture of sin as an entity. Before he commits murder, God visited Cain to warn him that "sin is crouching at the door; and its desire is for you, but you should rule over it."[8]

Through our human spirit we have access to the spirit world, of which Satan and his angelic realm as well as God and His host of heaven dwell in. Since man is the only creature that can access both worlds, Satan wants mans' access and authority to rule on earth. When Adam and Eve listened to Satan and disobeyed God, evil acquired its coveted access to them and their world.

1 John 5:19 says, "We know that we are of God, and the whole world lies under the sway of the wicked one." The wicked one is the evil, Lucifer, Satan, the dragon. No one is exempt from the wicked one's tempting, not even Jesus Christ. When Jesus went into the wilderness, before He began His ministry, the devil

tempted Him with several things, including 'all the kingdoms of the world.'[9] The devil claimed he could offer 'all the kingdoms of the world' because he had access to them; meaning, if Satan can rule in a man who rules a nation, or a company, or the media, etc., then Satan has access to the kingdoms of this world. It is, in fact, a legitimate claim.

THE CLASH OF TWO KINGDOMS

The fallout of Satan's scheming and Adam and Eve's disobedience resulted in the Bible's first recorded prophecy. This prophecy set the stage for a clash between two kingdoms: the Seed of God through the Adamic race and the seed of Satan.[10] Yes, according to Scripture, Satan can have seed:

> Now it came to pass, when men began to multiply on the face of the earth, and daughters were born to them, that the sons of God saw the daughters of men, that they were beautiful; and they took wives for themselves of all whom they chose.[11]

In Hebrew, the word for the sons of God is *HaElohim*, which is the word for angels. Jude 6 tells us there were angels that did not keep their abode; they noticed the daughters of men were lovely and they took them for themselves. The offspring of these angels and women produced giants, or "mighty men."[12] These mighty men or giants were also called "Nephilim."

These offspring were continually produced throughout time; Genesis 6:4 reads, "There were giants on the earth in those days, and *also afterward...*" (emphasis mine). "In those days" refers to the time pre-flood. "Also afterward" refers to the time post-flood.

We know Nephilim existed after the flood because Goliath was a nine-feet tall giant; he had four brothers that were also giants. Furthermore, David's court contained "mighty men," some of which fought in his army. According to Chuck Missler, several civilizations throughout history have legends similar to the Biblical account of the Nephilim:

> The idea that renegade angels came down to the earth and cohabited with women to produce a hybrid of offspring is pretty strange. But that notion is found in the legends of virtually every ancient culture on earth, including Sumer [where Iraq is today], Assyria, Egypt, the Incas, the Mayans, the Gilgamesh epic of Babylon, the Persians, Greece, India, Bolivia, South Sea Islands, and the Sioux Indians in the United States. They all have stories about 'star people' or gods of some kind who produced offspring on earth. [13]

Whenever Satan moves to destroy the image of God on earth—man—God moves in righteous anger to judge the adversary's work and to raise up an instrument of righteousness against it.

God's standard at that time was Noah; "But Noah found grace in the eyes of the Lord."[14] The flood, therefore, was a result of God's judgment upon the evil scheme of Satan.

TOWER OF BABEL

Some time after the flood, the next clash of the kingdoms occurs over an event called The Tower of Babel. Noah fathered three sons. One of them, Cush, fathered Nimrod. Nimrod's estate became the greatest in the world. At the time of his reign, the whole earth had one language, which I believe was Hebrew. Remember that God had given the mandate for man to multiply and subdue the earth;[15] well, Nimrod had other plans.

His name, Nimrod, means "we will rebel." Genesis 11:4 reads, "And they said, 'Come, let us build ourselves a city, and a tower whose top is in the heavens; let us make a name for ourselves, lest we be scattered abroad over the face of the whole earth.'"

A tower that reaches into the heavens symbolizes worship of the angelic realm. The word *name* is the Hebrew word *sem*, meaning "a manner or mark of confederation and organized unity." What Nimrod created is the Babylonian Religion. Because it is the cause for many conflicts between the kingdoms of darkness and light, it is important that we see the wickedness of this religion in order that we may understand God's judgment against it.

THE BABYLONIAN RELIGION

As king, Nimrod was worshiped as the sun-god, Bel (or, Baal). His wife's name, according to ancient writings, was Semiramis. Nimrod was a mighty hunter.[16] History tells us that he was killed in a hunting accident.

In those days, when the king died without a plan of succession, the ascender to the throne would kill the queen and the children—or take them as slaves in order to avoid an insurrection. To avert this, Semiramis claimed she was miraculously impregnated by a sunbeam that carried Nimrod's sperm. She named the child Tammuz.[17] In order to achieve the "miraculous," Semiramis acted in secret: Nimrod was not Tammuz's father; a lover unknown to Nimrod impregnated Semiramis. Impregnated with the son of a god, Semiramis is now worshiped as the Queen of Heaven.[18]

This account contains events counterfeit to those of Jesus Christ. For example, Semiramis' first conception was a counterfeit miraculous conception; also, because Nimrod's sperm was carried to Semiramis she was a counterfeit virgin. This account began a worldwide counterfeit religious system that revolved around the worship of a counterfeit mother, the "Madonna," and son. Various countries used different names.

Figure 2.1

Counterfeit Madonna and Child		
Country	**Mother**	**Child**
Egypt	Isis	Osiris
Assyria	Ishtar	Bacchus
India	Isi	Iswara
Asia	Cybele	Deoius
Greece	Aphrodite	Eros
Rome	Venus	Cupid

The most familiar counterfeit religious system originates with Constantine. In 312 A.D. Constantine brought the whole world under one rule and decided the Christian religion would be the one religion (he chose Christianity because one day during battle he saw a cross in the sky and claimed this to be his victory sign). He changed the names of Venus and Cupid to Mary and Jesus. Then, in 431 A.D., at the Counsel of Ephesus, the church declared the official worship of Mary and Jesus. It might sound innocent and traditional, but what is actually being worshipped is the Babylonian Religion. If you worship Mary and pray the rosary, you are worshipping the Queen of Heaven.

John mentions the Babylonian Religion in a letter he dictates for Jesus Christ to the church at Pergamos. He writes, "'I know your works, and where you dwell, where Satan's throne is.'"[19] The city of Pergamos worshipped the Babylonian Religion; as Christianity spread throughout the world, the priests and priestesses left Pergamos and went to Rome, where they established their religion. All the church did was change the names of the mother and son.[20]

While the worship rituals of these counterfeit religions may have differed, what remains unchanged is the fact that they are all traced back to Nimrod and his desire to build a city and a tower into the heavens.

WORSHIP AT THE ZIGGURAT

The Tower of Babel was built like a ziggurat, a rectangular shaped tower surmounted by a temple. The ziggurat is built in receding tiers; it has the form of a terraced pyramid. People stand at every level (tier) of the tower.

Thomas Cahill's book *The Gift of the Jews* describes how people actually worshiped the Babylonian gods. If they were worshipping a god (i.e., sun gods Baal or Tammuz; moon god Nanna-Sin) the temple was staffed with female priestesses. If they were worshipping a goddess, (i.e., Ashtoreth, Dinah) the temple was staffed with male priests. Regardless of the particular god being worshiped, both male and female prostitutes are used to "minister" to the gods. The early priests—predating Catholicism—were prostitutes. Cahill writes:

> Tonight is the night of the full moon; and, as darkness quickly falls and the moon rises in the heavens, we hear the sounds of hundreds of priestesses, chanting dully and playing primitive pipes and drums. Dressed in elaborate ceremonial garb, they gather solemnly around the terrace on which the temple is built, looking upward to the stepped pyramid beyond the temple, which rises almost in defiance of geometry, almost (it seems) to the sky itself. At the highest platform of this ziggurat (for so the stepped pyramid is called) is a small but glowing altar of lapis lazuli, carved fantastically with snakes and giant spiders, to

which an adolescent boy has been bound on his back. He is naked, though his flesh has been decorated in patterns of lozenges and zigzags to resemble the cobra. Priestesses of the highest order, also naked except for their extraordinary rings and spiral bracelets, are massaging the boy with gentle foreplay. As the moonlight illuminates his swelling member, the high priestess appears, as if from nowhere, dressed in a silver garment, which she sheds. Now naked, except for the myriad of pearls that decorate her body and painted spirals that adorn her breasts, she mounts the boy with the assistance of her sisters, who shriek their encouragement in a frenzy that only grows higher as the high priestess rides the boy, at first with rhythmic dignity, then with increasing agitation till her pearls tremble in the moonlight like so many miniscule planets, and the lozenges and spirals glisten, and both bodies, writhing in sweat, appear to be not so much earthly bodies as inhuman forces of the cosmos. All the priestesses, the lowest orders still on the terrace of the ziggurat's base, the higher orders arranged in ascending importance on the lofty steps of the ziggurat itself, are growing wild and ecstatic. Ripping open their robes and pawing themselves, they bay upward to the event on the ziggurat's height and to the moon itself. [21]

And then the boy dies. This is the kind of obscene and revolting worship that Satan created in order to defile man—the very man created in the image of God. Satan can't touch God, but he can touch the image of God—you. His desire is to defile you, take you as his prisoner, and make you his slave.

This is the religion that God abhors. It's not that He

hates the people, but the religion is hurting and perverting the people, so God must find others to go into the land of Canaan— the nucleus of this religion—and push the people out.

If God allowed Nimrod's desires to be fulfilled, if God did not order this religion to be stopped, this is the religion the multitudes would serve. The religion is not gone—people still serve this religion in bondage when they capture young girls and boys and put them in the slave trade (to give but one example of many horrible evils)—but God's actions will weaken the spread of the religion.

So once again, as God found Noah, God looks for a righteous man to be an instrument of righteousness upon the earth. This time He finds Abraham.

STUDY QUESTIONS

1. How does Satan and the kingdom of darkness gain access to believers?

2. What truths is Satan attempting to hide, cover, or twist?

3. Nimrod built Babel in order to "unify" mankind under one name, spreading false religion and idolatry. What are some examples of this scheme being used in our world?

4. How does understanding the Babylonian religion open your eyes to the world we now inhabit?

Chapter Three

FAMILY SECRETS

In the last chapter, you saw how civilization had become centered on the Babylonian Religion. God's response to this debasement was to come down and cause the people to speak in a multitude of languages, which disrupted the people's worship. It is out of this same area—Mesopotamia—that God called Abraham:

> Now the Lord had said to Abram: 'Get out of your country, from your family and from your father's house, to a land that I will show you. I will make you a great nation; I will bless you and make your name great; and you shall be a blessing. I will bless those who bless you, and I will curse him who curses you; and in you all the families of the earth shall be blessed.'[1]

Abraham is unique because he is the first recorded individual to leave the "circle of life" ideology and its worship of many gods to follow one God.[2] Even more astonishing for the time was Abraham's claim that this God speaks to man, a claim upon which Abraham stakes his life and the life of his family. The world at that time did not believe there was any god who would dwell with man. As 21st century Christians I don't think we can fully appreciate Abraham's decision to believe and follow one God as the God of their family—Abraham, Isaac, and Jacob.

God called Abraham at age 75 to leave his father's house and go west to a land he did not know, but was promised by God to be his inheritance. God's plans and purposes are secretly written into Abraham's family like a screenplay; thanks to Chuck Missler's work, those secrets are now uncovered.[3] The mystery of Christ can be seen in three events of the family of Abraham: the call of Abram, the sacrifice of Isaac, and the search for his bride. Their lives represent a type or shadow of things to come.

THE CALL

By faith Abraham obeyed when he was called to go out to the place which he would receive as an inheritance. And he went out, not knowing where he was going. By faith he dwelt in the land of promise as in a foreign country, dwelling in tents with Isaac and Jacob, the heirs with him of the same promise; for he waited for the city which has foundations, whose builder and maker is God...These all died in faith, not having received the promises, but having seen them afar off were assured of them, embraced them and confessed that they were strangers and pilgrims on the earth.[4]

Our calling is not too different than Abraham's. Just as God called Abraham out of a place that was enshrouded in darkness so that he might be the light of God, God is doing the same with you: "He has delivered us from the power of darkness and conveyed us into the kingdom of the Son of His love."[5] God first calls us out of the kingdom of darkness, the kingdom of Satan. He does not call us out of the world; He keeps us in the world and gives us instructions to not be a lover of the world.[6]

Before Abraham left for the city built by God, he dwelt in his father's house, which, at the time, was in a city ruled by the kingdom of darkness. Jesus spoke a similar message to the Pharisees, saying:

> You are of your father the devil, and the desires of your father you want to do. He was a murderer from the beginning, and does not stand in the truth, because there is no truth in him. When he speaks a lie, he speaks from his own resources, for he is a liar and the father of it.[7]

Like Abraham, we are called to leave the father of lies who tries to get us to believe that we are worthless and full of shame, leaving us to live a life of debauchery and shame. The father of lies uses the wounds we have carried to guide and direct our lives like a boat's rudder. Because the devil is a disembodied evil spirit recognized as a being, when he wants to influence us for his own schemes he connects with us through our spirit. Because we are spirit we hear these lies; if we give ear to them we become double-minded. We are called to serve only one God, not Him *and* the ruler of this world, but only the Lord God. It is this double-mindedness that we are called to leave behind and press onward to the upward call of God in Christ Jesus.

Furthermore, as Abraham was called to be a stranger and pilgrim on earth, so, too, are we: "For our citizenship is in heaven, from which we also eagerly wait for the Savior, the Lord Jesus Christ."[8]

The land Abraham sojourned in later became the Promised Land. Likewise, this earth that we are sojourners in will become the new heaven and new earth. And just as Abraham awaited a city whose foundations are built by God, so do we. This city is called Mt. Zion, which is another term for the eternal city, and throne room of God. For us this is a present as well as a future citizenship, since we are presently seated in the heavenly places in Christ Jesus.[9]

As it was for Abraham, so it is for us: the call to come out of our father's house has never changed. Abraham lived 3,500 years before Jesus Christ, yet his calling was the same as Paul's, Timothy's, the twelve disciples, and even ours.

THE SACRIFICE

After Abraham and Sarah conceived Ishmael by their own efforts, they conceived the son God had promised them— Isaac. At this point you will need to leave much of what you were taught in Sunday school behind. For starters, if you do the math you will discover that Isaac was not a young lad of 6 years, but of 33 years at the time he and Abraham climb the Mount chosen by God for his sacrifice. Abraham was 100 when Sarah conceived, and he is about 133 at the time he offers Isaac; meaning Isaac is about 33. In terms of Old Testament lifespan, 33 years is considered young, but it does not make him a little boy. Knowing Isaac's actual age is important because it coincides with Jesus' age at His time of ministry. There are more parallel facts and events between Isaac and Jesus; each event in Isaac's life is a type and foreshadow of Jesus Christ (see Figure 3.1).

Figure 3.1

Isaac as a "Type"	
Person/Event	Type
Isaac, age 33	Jesus, age 33
Abraham's only son, "whom you love"	God's only son (Col. 1:13, "son of His love")
Moriah, one of the mountains, name of which (vs. 14) means	"The Lord Will Provide"
Two servants	Two disciples
Donkey	Donkey
3 days' travel	3 days before Passover
Abraham places wood on Isaac's back	Jesus carries wooden cross on His back
Isaac is bound	Jesus is bound
"The lamb?" asks Isaac	"Behold, the Lamb of God Who takes away the sin of the world."
Unnamed servant, Eliezer (Gen. 15:3)	Holy Spirit, means "Comforter"
We read of Isaac again when he meets his bride, Rebekah	Jesus returns for His bride!

According to hermeneutics and the "law of first mention," the context and location of a word's first mention is important for its understanding. For example, when you do a word study, you need to find the original meaning of the word, which is found in the first place it is mentioned. The word could be mentioned 100 times and the meaning might change, or it might change according to Hebrew or Greek, but to understand the word's original meaning you trace it back to the place where it is first mentioned. The first time *love* is mentioned in the Bible is in this verse, Genesis 22:2, which reveals that Isaac is Abraham's only son, "whom you love," says God. This parallels with Jesus Christ because God says the "son of His love" is Jesus.

Next, the mountain where Abraham was called to take

Isaac was the same location in Jerusalem where Solomon later built the Temple. The city did not exist at the time of Abraham, but this mountain, Mt. Moriah, is where God sent Abraham. Today, under the gold Dome of the Rock in Jerusalem, you can see the rocky terrain of this mount. *Moriah* means "the Lord will provide."

Two servants and a donkey accompanied Abraham and Isaac on their three-day journey. Jesus entered Jerusalem, riding on a donkey, three days before Passover. When Jesus hung from the cross, there were only two disciples—John and his mother—present.

Isaac carried the wood for the sacrifice, similar to Jesus carrying His own cross. Note that if Isaac was six years old he would not have been strong enough to carry wood; however, if Isaac was 33 years old, as I believe he was, then he would have been strong enough. In Genesis 22:6-7, the wood is placed on Isaac. Isaac looks around, takes note of the fire and the wood, and inquires to the whereabouts of the lamb for the burnt offerings; in this era of history, animal sacrifice was understood and known to all, even Isaac. It was common knowledge that worshipping God required sacrificing a ram or a bull, which was far better (in God's eyes) than sacrificing a human being.[10]

Abraham responds to Isaac's inquiry by saying, "My son, God will provide for Himself the lamb for a burnt offering."[11] So Abraham and Isaac continued up Mt. Moriah and the servants stay behind. The chapter continues:

> Then they came to the place of which God had told him. And Abraham built an altar there and placed the wood in order; and he bound Isaac his son and laid him on the altar, upon the wood. And Abraham stretched out his hand and took the knife to slay his son. But the Angel of the Lord called to him from heaven and said, 'Abraham, Abraham!' So he said, 'Here I am.' And He said,

'Do not lay your hand on the lad, or do anything to him; for now I know that you fear God, since you have not withheld your son, your only son, from Me.' Then Abraham lifted his eyes and looked, and there behind him was a ram caught in a thicket by its horns. [12]

The lamb was slain in Isaac's place. Jesus, the "Lamb of God," was slain in our place. Although the aforementioned transpired between Abraham and Isaac, there was also a servant nearby. The servant is unnamed in this passage, however, in Genesis 15, the servant is called "Eliezer," whose name means "the comforter." Eliezer was Abraham's closest servant; in fact, when Abraham and Sarah still did not have the heir God promised, Abraham inquired of God if he was to bequeath his wealth to his servant, Eliezer, who had been a great comfort to him.[13] Symbolically, Eliezer represents the Holy Spirit, whom Jesus refers to as the Comforter.[14]

The final key event of Isaac's life is the answer to the question, "When do we read of Isaac again?" At the end of the sacrifice, Isaac is unmentioned. He is not mentioned again until he meets his bride, Rebekah, who is the third "type" mentioned in Isaac's story.

THE BRIDE

After the death of Sarah, Abraham decides Isaac needs a wife, so he instructs his oldest servant 'who ruled over all that he had' to go back to the land where he and Sarah came from and find a wife for Isaac. This servant must travel again through the Wilderness of Sin, whose people worshipped the moon god (where Allah is worshiped today), back to the old world, back to the father of lies, etc., back to what Abraham came out of! The servant is given a sign to recognize the woman: when she offers to draw water not just for him but also for all his camels, then he'll know she is the one to be Isaac's wife. Figure 3.2 shows the characters of the story and the "type" they represent.

Figure 3.2

Characters and their Type	
Character	**Represents**
Abraham	God; The "Ancient of Days" (Dan. 7:13)
Servant	Holy Spirit; Nameless, oldest
Rebekah	Bride
Isaac	Jesus

Genesis 24 has two main themes. The first is the responsibility of the servant (Holy Spirit) to go and get Rebekah (Bride); the second is the theme of the Bride (Rebekah) to willingly say "yes."

Once the servant recognizes Rebekah as the future bride, he meets her family and explains whom he works for and why he was sent. The servant presents the information in such a way that reveals he cannot force Rebekah to come with him, but he is asking her to make a decision. Figure 3.4 outlines the Scripture and events that take place.

Figure 3.3

Events in Genesis 24	
Scripture	**Event**
Gen. 24:1-10	The Holy Spirit's commitment to God's plan
Gen 24:11-32	Rebekah, a virgin, drawing water from a well
Gen 24:33-48	Holy Spirit reveals God's plan
Gen 24:49-60	The Bride's response: voluntary love
Gen 24:61-65	Fellowship with the Holy Spirit through wilderness journey
Gen 24:66-67	Consummation of the marriage in Sarah's tent: Isaac, the Son of God, with Rebekah, the Virgin. (Galatians 4:26)

To more fully understand the importance of the events, don't read them from a mindset of a Sunday school story, but prayerfully read them from a mindset of the responsibility of the Holy Spirit to go and secure the Bride. This is the same responsibility that the Holy Spirit still has today.

The Holy Spirit has been sent into the wilderness, into the land darkly inhabited by the father of lies; He is sent to draw us out (symbolic of Rebekah drawing the water). Only those who voluntarily chose to love God can be drawn out into a partnership where they will be formed into the Bride.

When Rebekah says "I will go"[15] she receives the following blessing: "Our sister, may you become the mother of thousands of ten thousands; and may your descendants possess the gates of those who hate them."[16] There are gates in the heavenlies between heaven and hell; there are gates between cities; and there are gates between regions. Rebekah and her descendants—including the children of Abraham, Isaac, and Jacob, and all those who believe by faith—will posses the gates of her enemies.

Following her "yes" to the Holy Spirit (servant), Rebekah is led by him all the way back through the wilderness of Sin into the promised land where Isaac awaits. We know that Abraham's servant brought treasures from his master's house and gave them to Rebekah, her brother, and her mother.[17] We can only imagine that along their journey together their conversations may have been laden with thoughts and words about Isaac and the kind of man he was. Could it not be that the servant's job is to make Rebekah feel comfortable and perhaps intimate with the man she is about to marry? For she is soon to meet him, as Scripture continues:

> And Isaac went out to meditate in the field in the
> evening; and he lifted his eyes and looked, and
> there, the camels were coming. Then Rebekah
> lifted her eyes, and when she saw Isaac she

dismounted from her camel; for she had said to her servant, 'Who is this man walking in the field to meet us?' The servant said, 'It is my master.' So she took a veil and covered herself. And the servant told Isaac all the things that he had done. Then Isaac brought her into his mother Sarah's tent; and he took Rebekah and she became his wife, and he loved her. So Isaac was comforted after his mother's death.[18]

This passage contains the second time the word *love* is used in the Bible. This is the marriage ceremony and the consummation of the marriage. The events of the passage represent the Holy Spirit coming down to the world of sin, of lies, of darkness, where He woos us and invites us to be partnered with Jesus Christ. He is our husband and we are called the Bride. There is an actual marriage supper of the Lamb that we will all partake in; it will be a wonderful time of union with the Lord. Right now we are only united in the spiritual realm, but He still views us as His Bride, making our pilgrimage toward Him, for He is coming again.

THE CHURCH: THE BRIDE FOR JESUS CHRIST

Rebekah represents the second picture of the Bride. The first picture is Eve, coming from the first Adam's side. The Bride today is the church, of which we are a part. Paul said, "For I am jealous for you with a godly jealousy. For I have betrothed you to one husband, that I may present you as a chaste virgin to Christ."[19] By this, Paul means that we are to love and serve one God. Paul accused Israel of being a harlot who prostituted herself to other gods; he felt it was his job to make sure the church is married only to Christ.

John the Baptist also presents the church to her husband,

"He who has the bride is the bridegroom; but the friend of the bridegroom, who stands and hears him, rejoices greatly because of the bridegroom's voice. Therefore this joy of mine is fulfilled."[20] John refers to Jesus Christ as the Bridegroom, and rightfully so as Jesus refers to Himself as the Bridegroom. Jesus saw Himself as the Bridegroom coming down to purchase the Bride.

In the Jewish tradition, the bridegroom would go to his bride-to-be's father seeking permission to be betrothed to his daughter. Then he would leave in order to get the house ready (traditionally, they would build an attachment on his own father's house). Similarly, Jesus, our Bridegroom, has left this earth saying 'In My Father's house there are many mansions.' Today He is making the house ready. And He's left the Holy Spirit to make us ready for Him.

The bride, after her engagement had been established, would leave her light on continually because she never knew when her betrothed would return. Similarly, we, the Bride, wait for our Bridegroom's unknown return when He will take us to His house and consummate the marriage in the Marriage Supper of the Lamb.

A PERFECT, UNIFIED BRIDE

God's original plan—before creation—was to have a suitable helpmate for Himself. Our God is love and therefore loves with great passion. In order to pour out His passion God needs an entity that will receive what He disperses. You and I are the object of that love. This is what motivates God to create one man, Adam, and then take Eve from his side.

The ultimate object of the Father's love is His Son; everything God does flows out to His Son and the Son returns this love back to Him. Because Christ opens the way to come to the Father He can birth many sons. The many sons become the perfect son, the one man in perfect unity that Jesus comes back for:

> For it was fitting for Him, for whom are all things and by whom are all things, in bringing many sons to glory, to make the captain of their salvation perfect through sufferings. For both He who sanctifies and those who are being sanctified are all of one, for which reason He is not ashamed to call them brethren. [21]

The many sons and Jesus the Son are one—having birthed you out of His side to give you Life—betrothing you to Himself, that together as one, all things in heaven and on earth will be united in Christ Jesus, for the glory of the Father.

THE BRIDAL CITY

The future for Christ and His Bride is a glorious one. Though Abraham never saw it in his lifetime, he beheld its glory in his spirit and believed God for the promise of it. In Revelation 21:2 the Apostle John is taken up to heaven and given a glimpse of what this glory will be like. John was shown a new heaven and a new earth: "Then I, John, saw the holy city, New Jerusalem, coming down out of heaven from God, prepared as a bride adorned for her husband." The saints in Christ Jesus are the Holy City, the New Jerusalem that will be the light of the new earth. This is God's inheritance in us, "the riches of His inheritance in the saints" and the "hope of His calling" that Paul wrote about.[22] This is God's blueprint from before time began. It is a love story from beginning to end, from Genesis to Revelation, and it is encoded into the family of Abraham as a picture of the Son of Man and His Bride.

But I am getting ahead of myself. Before the future glory

can be realized on earth as it is in heaven, the God of Abraham, Isaac, and Jacob must first make His name known among the people's of the earth. Let us see how God does this.

STUDY QUESTIONS

1. What does the call from the kingdom of darkness into the kingdom of light mean? Like Abraham, where will this call take you?

2. In your eyes, what is the most striking similarity between Jesus Christ and Isaac (the young man)? Why?

3. Knowing the first time the word *love* is written refers to a son, what does this say about God the Father? Further, what about the second reference to *love* being between Isaac and Rebekah, a man and his wife?

4. Parallel Rebekah's decision to say "yes" to Eliezar and travel with him to marry Isaac with our Christian walk of saying "yes" to the Holy Spirit, allowing Him to guide us on our journey on earth to meet Jesus Christ as a collective Bride.

5. What does God reveal about His eternal plan through the life of Abraham?

Chapter Four

"WHAT'S IN A NAME?"

The nation God first promised to Abraham eventually becomes quite large, and, unfortunately, in bondage to Egypt. When the cry of the people rises to heaven, God has already picked out His chosen vessel of honor: Moses. God finds Moses on the backside of the desert, where He reveals Himself to Moses in a burning bush as the God of Abraham, Isaac, and Jacob—the personal God of the family of Abraham. Moses is called to set the captives free and present instructions—God's plan of deliverance—to Israel's 70 elders.

When they follow these instructions their suffering labor is increased. Moses goes back to God and asks, "Lord, why have You brought trouble on these people? Why is it You have sent me?...You [have not] delivered Your people at all."[1] God answers by informing Moses that He has another name. 'What?! Disaster is at hand and you want to talk about a name change?' (At least this is what I would be thinking if I was in Moses' sandals.)

And God spoke to Moses and said to him: 'I am the LORD. I appeared to Abraham, to Isaac, and to Jacob, as God Almighty, but by My name LORD I was not known to them…And I have also heard the groaning of the children of Israel whom the Egyptians keep in bondage, and I have remembered My covenant. Therefore say to the children of Israel: 'I am the LORD; I will bring you out from under the burdens of the Egyptians, I will rescue you from their bondage, and I will redeem you with an outstretched arm and with great judgments. I will take you as My people, and I will be your God.'[2]

"I AM THE LORD"

I am wondering how a name could affect Pharaoh to the point where he decides to let God's people go. I think it has something to do with signs, wonders, and miracles—letting the world know He is bigger than the personal God of Abraham. Now He will show Pharaoh and Israel that He is God of heaven and earth. The stakes are much larger now.

God does indeed rescue them out of the hand of the Egyptian Pharaoh and brings them to Himself, to the mountain in the Wilderness of Sinai.[3] It is here at Mt. Sinai that God makes His plans to dwell among men; something He has not done since the Garden. God asks Moses to tell the people:

You have seen what I did to the Egyptians, and how I bore you on eagles' wings and brought you to Myself. Now therefore, if you will indeed obey My voice and keep My covenant, then you shall be a special treasure to Me above all people; for all the earth is Mine. And you shall be to Me a kingdom of priests and a holy nation.[4]

KINGDOM OF PRIESTS AND A HOLY NATION

Names give us our identity. Just as God's identity is larger than the personal family God of Abraham and is now reflected in His new title LORD, God moves to give His people a new name and new identity. By calling the people to be a kingdom of priests and a holy nation, God reveals how He intends for them to live before Him and before a watching world. No longer are they just the family of Abraham, but they are a holy nation, a nation that will be worthy of the respect of the world. No longer will the people relate to a "personal family God," but the LORD God of heaven and earth.

God's name and man's name are connected by their relationship to one another, meaning: if God is to dwell on earth among men and reveal Himself to the world, then the man in union with God needs to be holy, in order to minister before the Lord and before the world God's rule of heaven and earth. Francis Frangipane said, "That which God would empower He must first make holy."[5]

If God and man are to have a relationship, where will they meet? By choosing Mt. Sinai, I believe God revealed a type or shadow of a future meeting place—Mt. Zion, the heavenly city of the future, for she will rise above Jerusalem, and from there God in Christ will rule over the whole earth.

When I meditate on Exodus 19:10-11 I feel the excitement and anticipation of this meeting. God says to Moses, 'Tell them to get cleaned up, I'm coming in three days.'[6]

On the third day, Moses gathers what scholars believe to be about 3 million people, bringing them together at the base of Mt. Sinai to meet with God. Contrary to today's practice of being silent when preparing to meet God in a church building,

God comes with much fanfare—trumpets, thunder, lightning, fire, smoke, and shaking of the earth. Moses speaks and God answers him by voice.[7] The Lord comments on this later when He says, "You have seen that I have talked with you from heaven."[8] This was truly the grandest of all invitations! There were some rules to meeting God, like taking off your shoes and not touching things, but still, what an invitation.

I am saddened by the people's response, for while they accepted God's law, they rejected Him, saying, "[Moses], You speak with us, and we will hear; but let not God speak with us, lest we die."[9] What were they thinking? Fear. Almost all were thinking fear, save the 74 who met with God on the mountain. They ate and drank with Him and did not die.[10] However, because the majority of the people would not meet with God on the mountain as He planned, God persists and introduces another plan.

THE TENT OF MEETING

Through Moses, God asks the people if they will give an offering to make Him a sanctuary where He may dwell among them.[11] Expecting their answer to be affirmative, He gives Moses a list of housing needs, the most important item being the Ark:

> You shall put the mercy seat on top of the ark, and in the ark you shall put the Testimony that I will give you. And there I will meet with you, and I will speak with you from between the two cherubim which are on the ark of the Testimony, about everything which I will give you in commandment to the children of Israel.[12]

The Tent of Meeting is set up in the center of the

camp. The pillar cloud of smoke and fire that were on the mountain now enter the Tent and come to reside over the Ark of the Testimony—so called because the law, known as the Ten Commandments, was inside the gold covered box. We call this 'pillar' the Shekinah glory. Notice the law is present here just as it was on the mountain when God came to meet man.

As time goes by, God is provoked because the people have become "stiff-necked." Lest He consume them in His righteous anger, He orders Moses to move His Tent of Meeting outside the camp, knowing that those who do want to meet with God will have to walk for miles (which they do).[13] The cloud or pillar— the Shekinah glory—as the Presence of God became known, followed into the new location of the Tent. The nation of Israel followed this pillar of smoke and fire for the remainder of 40 years in the wilderness.[14]

However, because the people of Abraham as a whole reject God's original call to become a kingdom of priests and a holy nation, they restrict anyone who wants to meet with God from entering a tent, or a temple. And so God is limited to only one tribe (out of twelve) in the Nation of Israel that becomes priests and can enter the Holy of Holies. We see this mindset still today: we believe only a few people are deemed "holy" enough to become priests or pastors; furthermore, we erect buildings built by the hands of men in order to meet God.

But God still holds out hope for His plan of all His people being priests and kings. He shares His dream with the prophet Ezekiel. Speaking to the nation of Israel through Ezekiel He says:

> I will give you a new heart and put a new spirit within you; I will take the heart of stone out of your flesh and give you a heart of flesh. I will put My Spirit within you and cause you to walk in My statutes, and you will keep My judgments and do them.[15]

"THE LORD WHO DWELLS BETWEEN THE CHERUBS"

From the mountain to the Tent of Meeting, the Presence of God becomes solely identified with the Ark: God is referred to as "The LORD of hosts who dwells between the cherubim."[16] For almost 400 years God is known by this name.

During the time of Samuel the Judge, Israel goes to battle and they are near defeat. The Israelites bring the Ark onto the battlefield in hopes that His Presence will win them a victory.

In David's time, all that is left of the Tent of Meeting is the Ark of God. The Philistines take it for a while, but become desperate to give it back because it keeps causing their god (Dagon) to fall over. When David becomes king and establishes his throne in Jerusalem, he brings the Ark to the City of David. It still comes with rules of "don't touch"—that when ignored cause people's death—but King David wants it returned and, furthermore, he wants a temple built to house it. He draws up the plans, but his son Solomon builds it. Upon the Temple's completion and the arrival of 'moving day,' guess what appears that has not appeared for 400 years? The pillar cloud, the Shekinah glory, fills the House of God.[17] What a glorious day that must have been! Don't you wonder where the Shekinah glory is today?

THE HOLY SPIRIT IS THE *SHEKINAH* GLORY IN THE SAINTS

For God to be Lord of heaven and earth there has to be a place or housing that can hold His spirit and enthrone His ideals and purposes—His Lordship, if you will, on earth as it is already in heaven. In essence, He says, My Spirit, which was on the mountain, between the Cherubim, will move into you, born-again man. This word is fulfilled today in you and I. Jesus said,

> *"He who has My commandments and keeps them, it is*
> *he who loves Me. And he who loves Me will be loved*
> *by My Father, and I will love him and manifest Myself*
> *to him...and We will come to him and make Our home*
> *with him."*
> *John 14:21, 23*

The law is still the meeting place between God and man. The Shekinah glory in the Saints is where the law is *now* in the heart of man. Jesus did not abolish the law: He fulfilled the law according to Scripture:

> For what the law could not do in that it was weak through the flesh, God did by sending His own Son in the likeness of sinful flesh, on account of sin: He condemned sin in the flesh, that the righteous requirement of the law might be fulfilled in us who do not walk according to the flesh but according to the Spirit.[18]

Jesus Christ is the righteousness of God in us as He is the High Priest and Mediator of a better covenant.[19] The law of God in Christ is present every time our spirit man is in union with God's Holy Spirit. "The law of the Spirit of life in Christ Jesus has made me free from the law of sin and death."[20] So why do we keep resurrecting our own ways and means to meet God?

There is only one place to meet Him—in the Holy Spirit in our spirit. We are the temple of the living God, for God does not dwell in a temple built with hands.[21] Peter tells us, "But you are a chosen generation, a royal priesthood, a holy nation, His own special people, that you may proclaim the praises of Him who called you out of darkness into His marvelous light."[22]

What Israel rejected, God fulfilled anyway and is fulfilling even now until the end of the Church Age.

In the Revelation of Jesus Christ, which God gave Him to show His servants—the Church—we are given a glimpse of the throne room of heaven. And those around the throne sing to the Lamb of God Who sits at His right hand:

> You are worthy to take the scroll, and to open its seals; for You were slain, and have redeemed us to God by Your blood out of every tribe and tongue and people and nation, and have made us kings and priests to our God; and we shall reign on the earth.[23]

Even now as we see the Holy Spirit sanctifying us to be kings and priests unto God, there is still to come a time when Jesus Christ will establish His kingdom on earth in a real physical sense. Through the prophets we learn that the kingdom of God and Christ will be established on the earth in multiple phases. Let us turn now to the prophets and see how all of this will take place.

STUDY QUESTIONS

1. What difference does it make for God to be called "the God of Abraham, Isaac, and Jacob" or "the LORD"?

2. Names give us our identity. What names do you give yourself, and how does that identify you? (i.e. wife, lawyer, Presbyterian) What name has been placed on you by God? What about the name spoken concerning the church?

3. How do we limit God when we reject His call? Who else do we restrict in the process?

4. The Holy Spirit is deposited into a believer and each believer has the ability to know all things as the Spirit teaches the human spirit. What way(s) is this idea demonstrated or lacking within the church?

Chapter Five

GOD'S MYSTERY IN PROPHECY

"Surely the LORD God does nothing, unless He reveals
His secret to His servants the prophets."
Amos 3:7

Throughout the Old Testament, there are over 400 prophecies regarding Jesus Christ, all spoken by God's servants the prophets. These prophecies are mainly divided between two tracts of thought: One tract is Christ the suffering servant or Messiah; the second is Christ the reigning King who judges all the nations and rules the earth.

For example, John the Baptist, who is the last of the Old Testament prophets, said, "Behold, the Lamb of God who takes away the sins of the world."[1] Whereas Zechariah prophesied, "Rejoice greatly, O daughter of Zion! Shout!...Behold your King is coming to you...Lowly and riding on a donkey...His dominion shall be from sea to sea, and from the River to the ends of the earth."[2] The "anointed One" of Israel is *both* the Lamb and the King.

Since Jesus has already come and fulfilled His role as the Lamb, what will it mean for Him to come and fulfill His role as the King? God made a promise to David in 2 Samuel 7:13 that out of his seed will come a Son of God and "He shall build a house for My name, and I will establish the throne of his kingdom forever." The Lord God is very detailed, as we will see, in revealing to His prophets when and how the King and His kingdom shall come.

A BRIEF HISTORY

Following the establishment of Israel in the land of Canaan as a recognized nation, and many years of prosperity, the kingdom of priests that God first desired became a nation now ruled by kings, first Saul, then David. David's son Solomon built the House for God that David designed, but along the way he also built houses of worship for the pagan gods of his many wives as well. As God's Presence departed the Tabernacle, His main representation on earth became the Prophets. Through them God was able to make His voice heard. Sometimes the people listened, and many times they didn't. At times a king worshipped God solely, and at other times a king served several gods and polluted the land with idolatry. This idolatry weakened them as a nation, and they became an easy target for their enemies. God sent a warning through the prophets that an enemy was coming, and he indeed came.

Once the kingdom was divided in two and the northern tribe of Israel fell to the Assyrians, the Babylonians looked to take the southern tribe of Judah. The year is 605 B.C.; Daniel is a young man, age 16, taken into captivity along with others under the ruling leader of Babylon, Nebuchadnezzar.[3] The land is the same Mesopotamian region Nimrod ruled some 1500 years prior. The Baghdad of today sits 60 miles north of yesterday's Babylon.

NEBUCHADNEZZAR'S DREAM

King Nebuchadnezzar has a dream. He calls in his astrologers, magicians, and sorcerers, but none of them can interpret his dream. They tell the king, "There is no other who can tell it to the king except the gods, whose dwelling is not with flesh."[4] He is then told about a man, Daniel, taken from Judah into captivity, who can help. Nebuchadnezzar calls for Daniel, who tells the king:

> Blessed be the name of God forever and ever, for wisdom and might are His. And He changes the times and the seasons; He removes kings and raises up kings; He gives wisdom to the wise and knowledge to those who have understanding. He reveals deep and secret things; He knows what is in the darkness, and light dwells with Him. I thank You and praise You, O God of my fathers; You have given me wisdom and might, and have now made known to me what we asked of You, for You have made known to us the king's demand.[5]

As it was in Abraham's time, so it was in Daniel's: the philosophy of the world did not allow for a deity to dwell among men. But this was the God Daniel worshiped, the One who reveals deep and secret things to men. Upon giving the king the interpretation, the king responds by saying, "Truly your God is the God of gods, the Lord of kings, and a revealer of secrets, since you could reveal this secret."[6] God gave Nebuchadnezzar a vision of the coming rulers of the world; history proved Daniel's interpretation of the vision to be true. The vision is of a very tall giant clad in armor from the head to the legs, yet each part of the armor is made from a different metal. Daniel tells Nebuchadnezzar:

> The secret which the king has demanded, the wise men, the astrologers, the magicians, and the soothsayers cannot declare to the king. But there is a God in heaven who reveals secrets, and He has made known to King Nebuchadnezzar what will be in the latter days…You, O king, were watching; and behold, a great image! This great image, whose splendor was excellent, stood before you; and its form was awesome. This image's head was of fine gold, its chest and arms of silver, its belly and thighs of bronze, its legs of iron, its feet partly of iron and partly of clay. You watched while stone was cut out without hands, which struck the image on its feet of iron and clay, and broke them in pieces…And the stone that struck the image became a great mountain and filled the whole earth.
>
> This is the dream. Now we will tell the interpretation of it before the king. You, O king, are a king of kings. For the God of heaven has given you a kingdom, power, strength, and glory… But after you shall arise another kingdom inferior to yours; then another, a third kingdom of bronze, which shall rule over all the earth. And the fourth kingdom shall be as strong as iron, inasmuch as iron breaks in pieces and shatters everything; and like iron that crushes, that kingdom will break in pieces and crush all the others. Whereas you saw the feet and toes, partly of potter's clay and partly of iron, the kingdom shall be divided…And in the days of these kings the God of heaven will

> set up a kingdom which shall never be destroyed; and the kingdom shall not be left to other people; it shall break in pieces and consume all these kingdoms, and it shall stand forever. Inasmuch as you saw that the stone was cut out of the mountain without hands, and that it broke in pieces the iron, the bronze, the clay, the silver, and the gold—the great God has made known to the king what will come to pass after this. The dream is certain, and its interpretation is sure.[7]

The first kingdom, whose head is of gold, represents the Babylonian Empire, which Nebuchadnezzar ruled, thereby holding Israel in captivity.

The second kingdom, whose arms and chest are made of silver, represents Nebuchadnezzar's successors, King Darius the Mede, and King Cyrus of Persia; they usher in what is known as the Medo-Persia Empire. Daniel is alive during this time, because it is still during the 70 years of Israel's captivity.

The third kingdom, whose belly and thighs are of bronze, represents the Grecian Empire. Other important names of this period are Alexander the Great, Antiochus Epiphanes, and the first book of Maccabees (the Maccabees cover the 400 years between the Old and New Testaments. If you have a Catholic Bible, you have books 1 and 2 Maccabees).

The fourth kingdom, whose legs are of iron, represents the Roman Empire that reigned at the time of the New Testament. As you know, today the Roman Empire[8] no longer rules, and the world is divided into different nations and states. But before Christ comes back, before the world leader that occupies "center stage," the world will be divided into ten powerhouses—represented by the 'ten toes.'

Just as Daniel prophesied, these kingdoms did dominate the world, as history confirmed.

Figure 5:1

Rulers of the World		
King.	**Represented by**	**Meaning**
1st	Head of gold	Babylonian Empire
(70 yrs of Jewish captivity)		
2nd	Chest & arms of silver	Medo-Persia Empire
(book of Esther)		
3rd	Belly & thighs of bronze	Grecian Empire
(Alexander the Great; Antiochus Epiphanes; 1 Maccabbes 1-6)		
4th	Legs of iron	Roman Empire
(toes of the feet, iron and clay, vs. 42-45)		

Nebuchadnezzar's successor is Belshazzar. During his reign, Daniel receives both a vision, and Gabriel's interpretation, of four beasts that rise out of the earth (Daniel 7). The beasts represent the four kingdoms of the previous vision, but in more detail, especially concerning the fourth kingdom. During the time of the fourth kingdom, ten kings ('ten toes') shall rise up; these are the "powerhouses," as I call them. These powerhouses will dominate the world; however, towards the end of time, one 'horn,' or king, will rise out of the ten speaking "pompous words against the Most High."[9] Then, says Gabriel:

> The kingdom and dominion, and the greatness
> of the kingdoms under the whole heaven, shall be
> given to the people, the saints of the Most High.
> His kingdom is an everlasting kingdom, and all
> dominions shall serve and obey Him.[10]

What does it mean for the kingdom of God to be given to the Saints? Remember, earlier Gabriel told Daniel:

*"In the days of these kings the God of heaven will set up
a kingdom which shall never be destroyed."*
Daniel 2:44

Through Daniel's prophecies we see there is a time to establish the kingdom and there is another time to give the kingdom, as an inheritance, to the saints of the Most High. These are two different times (which I will discuss further in chapter 7). Gabriel, in his next vision to Daniel, reveals a timeline of events for these two different times—the establishing and the inheriting of this kingdom. It is called the Seventy Weeks of Daniel. I want to thank Chuck Missler for his work in uncovering this mystery.[11]

SEVENTY WEEKS OF DANIEL

Seventy weeks are determined for your people and for your holy city, to finish the transgression, to make an end of sins, to make reconciliation for iniquity, to bring in everlasting righteousness, to seal up vision and prophecy, and to anoint the Most Holy. Know therefore and understand, that from the going forth of the command to restore and build Jerusalem until Messiah the Prince, there shall be seven weeks and sixty-two weeks; the street shall be built again, and the wall, even in troublesome times. And after the sixty-two weeks Messiah shall be cut off, but not for Himself; and the people of the prince who is to come shall destroy the city and the sanctuary. The end of it shall be with a flood, and till the end of the war desolations are determined. Then he shall confirm a covenant with many for one week; but in the middle of the week he shall bring an end to sacrifice and offering. And on the wing of abominations shall be one who makes desolate, even until the consummation, which is determined, is poured out on the desolate.[12]

At the time Daniel received this vision, the yearly calendar recorded 300 days, not 365 days; it was a 12-month, 30-day calendar, which the Romans later changed. Also, it was common knowledge in Daniel's era to know that seven years equals one "week" (similar to our understanding that 10 years equals one "decade"). Therefore, when we're talking about 69 weeks, we actually mean 69 seven-year periods.

Figure 5.2

The Seventy Weeks of Daniel				
Commandment to rebuild Jerusalem by decree of Artaxerxes Longimanus March 14, 44 BC	Messiah the King, His Triumphal Entry April 6, 32 AD	Interval	70th Week (Abomination of Desolation)	The Great Tribulation (Rev. 6-19)
└──── 69 Weeks ────┘ (69 x 7 x 360 = 173,880 days)				

This revelation is for the end time, in which we currently live. Gabriel tells Daniel that from the time there is a commandment to rebuild Jerusalem to the time it is finished will be seven weeks. After the seven weeks, there will be 62 more weeks until "Messiah shall be cut off," meaning, the Crucifixion. These first 69 weeks have already occurred; we can count them according to historical events.

Artaxerxes Longimanus[13] gave a decree on March 14, 445 B.C. to rebuild the temple. The date Jesus rode a donkey into Jerusalem was April 6, 32 A.D. If you count the years from 445 B.C. to 32 A.D. (knowing there is no year "0", you subtract 1), you get 476.

$$445 + 32 - 1 = 476$$

Then, to convert to the Julian calendar, introduced by Julius Caesar in 46 BC, multiply the number of days by 365 days in a year.

$$476 \times 365 = 176,740$$

Next, subtract the days from March 14 to April 6, for a total of 24 days. Add this to the previous number.

$$24 + 173,740 = 173,764$$

Then we have to factor in Leap years, of which there are 116.

$$116 + 173,764 = 173,880$$

Therefore, the total number of days from the time Artaxerxes Longimanus gave the decree to rebuild the temple to the day Jesus rode into Jerusalem was 173,880 days.

If you refer back to Daniel's vision, he knew this time period would last 69 weeks. If Gabriel's interpretation is accurate, this time period should be 173,880 days. Is it?

Because one week is seven years, multiply 69 x 7.

$$69 \times 7 = 483$$

Because Daniel lived before the Julian calendar, multiply

the number of days by 360 days in a year.

$$483 \times 360 = 173{,}880$$

Again, the number of days from the commandment to rebuild Jerusalem to the number of days Jesus entered Jerusalem are 173,880, which is the exact amount of days Gabriel told Daniel that it would be. How would Jesus have known to enter Jerusalem exactly 173,880 days after the decree? Because this day had been prophesied about. And Jesus had access to the same prophetic word that we do, so He was able to know the exact day in which He was to enter Jerusalem and show Himself as King.

THE TRIUMPHANT ENTRY

Jesus' Triumphant Entry is recorded in Luke 19:38, 41-44. The people proclaim:

> Blessed is the King who comes in the name of the Lord! Peace in heaven and glory in the highest!'... Now as [Jesus] drew near, He saw the city and wept over it, saying, 'If you had known, even you, especially in this your day, the things that make for your peace! But now they are hidden from your eyes. For days will come upon you when your enemies will build an embankment around you, surround you and close you in on every side, and level you, and your children within you, to the ground; and they will not leave in you one stone upon another, because you did not know the time of your visitation.'

I think it is important to recognize that the specific time

prophesied by Daniel is not the day of Jesus' crucifixion, but the day of His coming to Jerusalem as a King. The focus is on His Kingship—His rule and reign—not on His death. At no other time but this day did Jesus allow the people to call him King. Previously, when Jesus performed miracles the people would say, "Is this the one? Is this the Messiah?" People wanted to make Him a king, but every time they clamored to call Him "King" Jesus forbid them. And yet on this day Jesus not only allows it, but also tells the disciples to arrange it.[14] Why is this day more significant than any other? Because it is the day of His anointing as Messiah the Prince, and if He is first a Prince, then one day He will be King.

THE 70TH WEEK

Daniel's prophecy states seventy weeks are determined "to make an end of sins, to make reconciliation for iniquity, to bring in everlasting righteousness, to seal up vision and prophecy, and to anoint the Most Holy."[15] The week of the Passion of Jesus Christ accomplished one half of the proclamation and marked the end of the 69th week with the "cutting off of the Messiah." Yet Daniel was given a prophecy regarding 70 weeks, which means there is one more week—7 years—that have yet to be fulfilled and "seal up the prophecy and anoint the Most Holy."

The 70th week is described in Daniel 9:27 and also in Matthew 24:15-16. In Matthew, Jesus is speaking to His disciples. He says, "Therefore when you see the 'abomination of desolation,' spoken of by Daniel the prophet, standing in the holy place' (whoever reads, let him understand), 'then let those who are in Judea flee to the mountains.'"

The last of the seven years, the 70th week of Daniel, begins with a world leader signing a fully accepted peace treaty with the Jews; it does not begin with the rapture of the Church.

(Regarding the rapture, there is no pending prophecy for its fulfillment; therefore, it could happen at any time.)

The covenant of peace made with Israel is broken half way through the 70th week when the one world leader makes a demand from a wing in the Jerusalem Temple that he will be worshiped by the whole world. This is the aforementioned "abomination of desolation," for when this happens, two-thirds of the Jews are killed. That is why the last three and half years of this 7th week are called the Tribulation. At the end of the Tribulation, Jesus will come, arrayed in the glory of a King with His Bride, and begin His Millennial reign over the nations from Jerusalem.

THE 'AGE' OF THE CHURCH

But before the dawn of the seven-year period, there is an interval of time. This is the time in which we are currently living; it is called the "Age of the Church." Paul mentions this interval in a letter to the Romans,

> What if God, wanting to show His wrath and to make His power known, endured with much longsuffering the vessels of wrath prepared for destruction, and that He might make known the riches of His glory on the vessels of mercy, which He had prepared beforehand for glory, even us whom He called, not of the Jews only, but also of the Gentiles? As He says also in Hosea: 'I will call them My people, who were not My people, and her beloved, who was not beloved. And it shall come to pass in the place where it was said to them, "You are not My people," There they shall be called sons of the living God.'[16]

Paul, repeating the words of the prophet Hosea, reminds the Romans that there will be a people who are not just His people—Israel—but there will come a time when the Gentiles will also be His people. Paul received revelation from the Holy Spirit regarding the "mystery of the church"[17] and how she will be an heir to the promised inheritance along with the Jews. It is during this time of approximately 2,000 years that the church of Jesus Christ is being built for "a dwelling place of God in the Spirit."[18]

Establishing the kingdom of God on earth is a process that began with the first coming of Christ. The kingdom continues to be built during the 'age' of the Church until Christ comes the second time to give the kingdom as an inheritance to the saints who suffered for her to be built up, overcoming the enemy. They—the saints—will rule with Christ during His millennial reign on earth.

Because this interval of time between the 69th and 70th weeks of Daniel's prophecy is the church age, it is my opinion that if you want to know where we are in relation to end-time events, you should pay careful attention to two things: study the condition of the church, rather than eschatology, and study what is happening in modern day Israel. These two issues are the most important. Jesus comes back to take unto Himself a church that is mighty in power, ready to rule and reign with Him, not a church that is sitting here waiting to be raptured. As for Israel, the tribulation years will have her crying out for her Savior, the Lord Jesus Christ, only this time, she will recognize Him when He comes.

Remember that although Israel will recognize Christ at His second coming, they did not recognize Him at His first visitation even though Jeremiah prophesied:

> 'Behold, the days are coming,' says the LORD,
> 'that I will perform that good thing which I have
> promised to the house of Israel and to the house

of Judah: In those days and at that time I will cause
to grow up to David a Branch of righteousness;
He shall execute judgment and righteousness in
the earth.'[19]

And Isaiah prophesied:

For unto us a Child is born, unto us a Son is given;
and the government will be upon His shoulder...
Of the increase of His government and peace
there will be no end, upon the throne of David
and over His kingdom, to order it and establish it
with judgment and justice from that time forward,
even forever.[20]

The promise of God to establish a King on David's throne
Who will establish righteousness in this world is what Paul calls
the gospel of God.[21] And so when God's appointed time came,
He sent His Son into the world, with power according to the
Holy Spirit, to preach the message we know as the gospel of the
kingdom of God.

STUDY QUESTIONS

1. What assurance or hope is there in knowing God reveals secrets?

2. How is God, right now, setting up a kingdom that will never be destroyed?

3. What mindsets must shift in order to understand that the kingdom of God is both heaven and earth? Now and future? How do you currently view the earth?

4. What greater power have we not realized in the Lord's prayer? (i.e. "Thy Kingdom come, Thy will be done on earth as it is in heaven.")

5. King Jesus established His throne with justice and righteousness. What stops us from joining with Him and praying for the kingdom to be established here on earth this day?

PART II

THE MYSTERY MANIFESTED BY JESUS CHRIST

*"God, who at various times and in various ways
spoke in time past to the fathers
by the prophets, has in these last days
spoken to us by His Son,
whom He has appointed heir of all things,
through whom also He made the worlds."*
Hebrews 1:1-2

Chapter Six

THE GOSPEL OF THE KINGDOM OF GOD

God spoke through His prophets about a day when His "anointed One" of Israel would come. John the Baptist was called by God to prepare the way for this day. When it finally arrived, Jesus the Son of Man proclaimed its arrival and began to establish the kingdom of God in the world through His disciples and then His body, the Church. Indeed, it would be as the LORD God desired: a kingdom of priests and a holy nation.

THE DAY OF PROCLAMATION

Following Jesus' baptism by John the Baptist and his subsequent 40 days of trial in the wilderness, Jesus "returned in the power of the Spirit to Galilee."[1] In His hometown of Nazareth He enters the synagogue on the Sabbath and stands up to read from the book of Isaiah,

The Spirit of the Lord is upon me, because He has anointed me to preach the gospel to the poor; He has sent me to heal the brokenhearted, to proclaim liberty to the captives and recovery of sight to the blind, to set at liberty those who are oppressed; to proclaim the acceptable year of the Lord.[2]

After reading from Isaiah, Jesus says, "Today this Scripture is fulfilled in your hearing." At first the people marvel, but then they are stirred to wrath and try to throw Him over a cliff. Who would stir up such wrath? Satan, of course, for his kingdom of darkness has just been invaded by the kingdom of God. Jesus moves throughout Galilee to heal and deliver people from the sickness and demonic oppression of Satan. This is the same region of Israel that Isaiah the prophet had prophesied about: out of the land of Zebulun and Naphatali, in the Galilee of the Gentiles, "The people who sat in darkness have seen a great light, and upon those who sat in the region and shadow of death Light has dawned."[3]

Pressed by people to stay in Galilee, Jesus replies, "I must preach the kingdom of God to the other cities also, because for this purpose I have been sent."[4]

I believe there is a great need in the church today to rediscover the message and purpose of Jesus Christ. Paul said that his gospel and the preaching of Jesus Christ were both "according to the revelation of the mystery kept secret since the world began."[5] Paul and Jesus called this message the gospel of the kingdom of God.

THE KINGDOM OF GOD

In 1996, while recovering from major surgery, I heard the Spirit of the Lord say to me, "Get out of the man-built kingdom."

My thought at the time was that *kingdom* was a strange word to use since we are past the era of the Medieval Ages. Prior to the surgery I had been very active in several ministries that now were put aside for the year so I could recover. During this time I read the complete works of Francis Schaeffer. My evangelical world was turned upside down as I realized the gospel according to Jesus and Paul was built upon the demonstration of the rule of God in Christ over the rule of Satan. It was and is a gospel of power to heal and deliver—to set the captives free. Contrasting this with the evangelical gospel of grace and positive-thinking motivational sermons, I began to see that man had built something in place of God's rule and reign.

I believe it's time for the church to have a discussion regarding this matter. The gospel of grace centers on a 'born-again' message, Jesus as Savior, and revival theology. It leaves me with an identity of a sinner saved by grace. This identity is a half-truth that leaves the door wide open to fallacies about who I am in Christ. Like the AA program for alcoholics, I am forever bound to my identity as one with my disease. Contrast this with the gospel of the kingdom of God where, by faith, I receive Christ as Lord. His resurrected life in me rules over the work of Satan; I am healed, delivered, and called to set others free, just as I have been. I am a witness to the kingdom of God and the rule of Christ.

Kingdom implies that there is a Lord or King. One day, out of curiosity, I counted how many times *Savior,* and *Lord* or *King* were used in the New Testament in reference to Jesus Christ. The answer was 9 to 365 plus, the winner being by far "Lord or King." The modern Christian uses both *Lord* and *Savior* as one and the same, but I believe they are mostly ignorant of the difference or else they would see power in their lives over the works of the devil, for that is what the gospel of the kingdom of God promises to those who believe. Believe to the extent of living a life that demonstrates Jesus as Lord.

Because the church preaches and teaches only a half

gospel she is weak in her power and in her witness. The traditional evangelical paradigm is power for salvation, witnessing, and holy living. The message is "God loves, Jesus saves, be blessed!" The witness is our personal testimony of salvation.

Whereas the gospel of the kingdom paradigm is power to destroy the works of the devil: sin, sickness and death. The message is "Repent, for the rule of God in Christ is here." The witness is our testimony to the power of the broken body and shed blood of Jesus to heal and to deliver.

George E. Ladd, formerly of Fuller Theological Seminary, wrote this in 1959: "The Kingdom of God is a miracle. It is the act of God. It is supernatural. Men cannot build the kingdom, they cannot erect it. God has entrusted the Gospel of the Kingdom to men. It is our responsibility to proclaim the Good News about the Kingdom, but the actual working of the Kingdom is God's rule and reign."[6]

If we believe God's power to heal and deliver ended with the New Testament church, then we are only left with activities to keep us in fellowship and busy until Christ comes for us. Our good intentions to live like Christ are reduced to man attempting to live out of his soul what God promised from His Spirit.

For both Jesus and Paul, the gospel was a message preached by the demonstration of power, not just in words. Jesus said,

> *"If I cast out demons by the Spirit of God, surely the kingdom of God has come upon you."*
> *Matthew 12:28*

> *"My speech and my preaching were not with persuasive words of human wisdom, but in demonstration of the Spirit and of power."*
> *1 Corinthians 2:4*

If the demonstration of the power of God is the gospel,

then what is declared? The kingdom of God, the kingdom of light, has come to establish itself against the kingdom of darkness. Jesus said He came to bring a sword.[7] A sword against whom? The Devil; Satan. He is the evil one who imprisons the hearts, minds, and bodies of men, whom God created in His likeness and called to bear forth the image of God before the world. Not only does man need to be redeemed, he will need to be empowered by God's own life in order to live as a witness to the gospel of the kingdom of God. The kingdom of God is the rule of heaven on earth. In heaven there are no mental illnesses, addictions, or diseases. Hurting people with shattered lives are crying out to God. His answer was then, and is today, the church. Why then is she so powerless? She's not powerless all over the world; in the southern hemisphere where the gospel of the kingdom of God is preached she is showing herself to be strong;[8] but in North America and in Europe she is weak.

I believe there are two reasons for weakness in the northern hemisphere churches. First, there is a lack of knowledge and understanding of the complete purposes for which Christ came; and second, there is far too little of the life of the Holy Spirit being lived out through the church. But the world is waiting!

THE PURPOSES OF JESUS

When Jesus said that He came "to finish the work of the Father,"[9] we must ask ourselves "What work did God the Father start that the Son was sent to complete?" This is why we studied the Old Testament, to see that the Father's will was to establish Himself on earth as He is in heaven. Remember, His name is LORD God of heaven and earth. His chosen vessel to inhabit was Man; therefore, the Son of Man was sent to complete this work. But because man is now with sin, there were two things that Christ had to accomplish. The first was to make the payment for sin, so that the second—the establishing of the kingdom of

God on earth as it was in heaven—could progress, as planned from the beginning of time.

Breaking the power of sin over our lives was the first order of business. Sin came in to the world, and by it all the world was held captive to its power, until Jesus, the Son of Man, came and broke its power. Jesus initially broke sin's power by His death, which was a payment for sin, "having wiped out the handwriting of requirements that was against us," and broke sin's power again by His resurrection, "having disarmed the principalities and powers"[10] through which Satan ruled; sin's power has now been broken for eternity!

Jesus' second order of business was to establish the kingdom of God on earth. This He did by first declaring with demonstration that it was here, and then by inviting others—first His disciples and then 70 others—to participate in the work of the kingdom.[11]

Then, following His resurrection, He promised and delivered the Holy Spirit to the disciples, by whom He was anointed to do the works of the kingdom. Then Jesus commissioned the disciples to do the same works, and even greater, until He comes back.[12]

As demonstrated by Christ, the kingdom of God can only be experienced by the life of the Holy Spirit.

ANOINTED BY THE HOLY SPIRIT

Jesus walked out of the wilderness and into the synagogue "in the power of the Spirit." Why would Jesus, the Son of God, need the power of the Holy Spirit? The answer is simple: for healing and miracles. We must understand that as the Son of man, Jesus left His divine nature in heaven. He was tempted many times to access His deity, but in obedience to the Father,

He laid it down, took on the form of man, and became obedient to the point of death.[13] Describing His life, Jesus said,

> *"No one takes it from Me, but I lay it down of Myself.*
> *I have power to lay it down, and I have power to take it*
> *again. This command I have received from My Father."*
> *John 10:18*

If Jesus could not call on the divine nature He left behind, what power did He call on? Acts 10:38 reads, "God anointed Jesus of Nazareth with the Holy Spirit and with power, who went about doing good and healing all who were oppressed by the devil, for God was with Him." Jesus accessed power from heaven through the Holy Spirit—the same power available for us today.

Classic Christian theology allows us an excuse for not pressing in to the full gospel of the kingdom by assigning a dual nature to Jesus: human and divine, man and deity. Like a remote control we 'click' back and forth between His divine and human natures whenever it is convenient for us. I say *convenient* because if I believe Jesus performed healing and miracles from His divine nature, but preached and fellowshipped from His human nature, then I am absolved from having to fulfill the whole commission of Christ; for I do not have His power or authority to do healing and miracles, since He did these as God.

On the contrary, Jesus was just as dependent upon the Holy Spirit as you and I are. The only difference between Him and us is that His DNA was from God and ours is from men and women with sin. Therefore, He was without sin and we are not. Nothing is impossible with God. If God could form man out of dust, then it is entirely plausible for God to form a man in Mary's womb without any of her DNA.

Knowing His disciples would need the same indwelt life of God for them to fulfill His commission to go into the world preaching the gospel of the kingdom of God, teaching repentance and remission of sins, and baptizing in His name all who would believe, Jesus said,

> *"Behold, I send the Promise of My Father upon you; but*
> *tarry in the city of Jerusalem until you are endued with*
> *power from on high."*
> *Luke 24:49*

The Promise of His Father is the Holy Spirit. Jesus said, "When He, the Spirit of truth, has come, He will guide you into all truth; for He will not speak on His own authority, but whatever He hears He will speak; and He will tell you things to come. He will glorify Me, for He will take of what is Mine and declare it to you."[14]

And this is exactly what He did. After He rose from the dead He appeared to the disciples, for they had followed His instructions to wait in Jerusalem; Jesus said,

> *"Peace to you! As the Father has sent Me, I also send*
> *you." And when He had said this, He breathed on them,*
> *and said to them, "Receive the Holy Spirit."*
> *John 20:21-22*

Just as the Lord of heaven and earth breathed His life into the first man—Adam—the Lord again breathes His life into born-again man and says, 'receive My Spirit.'

It is my desire that you understand this, for "the kingdom of God is in you."[15] The key to experiencing this power is to live your life under the governance of God in the Holy Spirit; this is why Jesus and Peter preached repentance.

REPENTANCE

"Repent, for the kingdom of heaven is at hand," Jesus said.[16]

But Peter said it differently, "Repent, and let every one of you be baptized in the name of Jesus Christ for the remission of sins; and you shall receive the gift of the Holy Spirit."[17] The requests for repentance differ because Jesus had not yet been crucified and resurrected, so he announced that it was near; however, at the time of Peter's sermon, Jesus (as the last Adam) had become a life-giving Spirit, so Peter could offer both repentance and baptism into the life of God—the gift of the Holy Spirit. Repentance and confession that "Jesus is Lord" opens the way for the Life of God in Christ to enter man's spirit and make it alive and accessible to the God of heaven and earth.

Repent means to turn from, go in another direction. To embrace the kingdom I must also be willing to embrace the Lord's rule over my life. I must turn from my self-rule and self-interests to the governance of the Holy Spirit.

This is where spiritual vision is important. If I only see the blessings of God that come my way as a "saved" member of the family of God, and miss seeing His inheritance in me as His chosen vessel for His Presence on earth, I most likely will not be motivated to give up my self-rule for His. But, if I see that all are not equal in heaven and that those who work in the family business of building the kingdom of God receive a bridal inheritance, then the immediate verses long-term rewards of God become an eternal issue.

Perhaps if we knew historically how the Godhead purposes to establish the kingdom of God it would help us to see things differently. Like a symphony, the kingdom of God was planned by the Godhead to be established on the earth in three movements.

THE KINGDOM OF GOD ESTABLISHED IN THREE PHASES

The first movement occurred 2,000 years ago at Jesus'

initial coming to earth, whereby He declared in demonstration that the kingdom of God was here. This was first announced to the Jews. Later, the Apostles expanded the message to include the Gentiles; those who became disciples of Jesus Christ spread the message throughout the world and continue to do so as we live out the Church Age.

The second movement begins at His return, His second coming, which follows after the Tribulation, or great persecution at the end of the current age. At this time Jesus will establish His Millennial reign on the earth from Jerusalem, where He will rule with His Bride. During this time Satan is bound and can neither influence nor harm man. Also during this time, the earth will undergo a period of restoration. At the end of the 1,000 years Satan is loosed, and there is one last battle called Armageddon; Christ is the Victor, and Satan is sent to Hell for eternity. Jesus hands His kingdom, also known as the "kingdom of heaven," to His Father, and now the last movement begins.

In this last phase, out of the fire and destruction of the current earth[18] the new heavens and earth are created. At this time, the Book of Life, the Father's book, is opened before the great white judgment seat of God.[19] This book is heaven's record of each person's individual response to who they said God's Son is and whether they received him by faith. All those whose names are listed in the book will live in the new heavens and earth. All those who are not in the book will join Satan and his angels in hell's fire.[20] John describes the event in Revelation 21:2, "the holy city, New Jerusalem, coming down out of heaven from God, prepared as a bride adorned for her husband."

As God the Father has a book, so does Jesus the Son; His book is called the Lamb's book of life.[21] The names recorded in Jesus' book, the Lamb's book, are those of the Bride. Thus, the kingdom of God with the kingdom of Christ is now completely and fully established in heaven and on earth.[22]

Just to clarify, many people today believe that when they die they immediately go to the new heavens and earth of

Revelation 21 and 22, but this is not true, for the new heavens and new earth have not yet been created. First, the Bride must be chosen.

CHOOSING THE BRIDE

Until Jesus returns we are living in what is called the Church Age, which is part of the first phase. Here the kingdom of God is established on earth through the Church, the body of Christ. As the body of Christ we are to do the same works that Jesus did: heal the sick, deliver the oppressed, and preach the gospel. As we do this, adding daily to the kingdom those who believe upon the name of Jesus Christ, the kingdom of God is built. Out of this, the kingdom of God, Jesus will choose for Himself a Bride, and she is called the kingdom of heaven (or, the kingdom of Christ). Jesus went to great lengths to teach the disciples this, as we will see in the next chapter.

At the end of the Tribulation Jesus returns with the Bride, and they will rule and reign together for 1,000 years. Jesus' glorious 'touch down' is depicted by the prophet Zechariah.[23]

"And in that day His feet will stand on the Mount of olives, which faces Jerusalem on the east...Thus the Lord my God will come, and all the saints with You."
Zechariah 14:4-5

Without a vision of her future glory, and the responsibility to ensure it by faith, the Church has settled for half of the gospel. Out of ignorance and self-love she sits, waiting for her Savior to rapture her, without the slightest idea that when He does, she will come before the judgment seat of Christ and have to give an account of her works. The judgment seat of Christ is separate from the great white throne of God's judgment. The works being judged by Christ are not works for salvation, for salvation is the free gift of God to all those who believe in Jesus Christ. No, these are works that qualify her to be rewarded with an inheritance in the kingdom of Christ or heaven. As Jesus said to John, "He who overcomes shall inherit all things, and I will be His God and he shall be My Son."[24] Those who inherit the kingdom of Christ are also inheritors of the kingdom of God. There are two inheritances; the gift of eternal life is one, and the inheritance in the kingdom of the Son is another.

TWO INHERITANCES

Dale Sides, president of Liberating Ministries for Christ International, teaches it this way:

> There are two separate kingdoms and an inheritance for each one...God the Father has a kingdom over which He will rule (Revelation 21-22). In this kingdom, His grace will be equally divided to all of His children (Revelation 21:7). He has been, is now, and will at that time be, no respecter of persons. Jesus the Messiah also has a kingdom where He will sit on the throne of His Father and will rule over the earth with a rod of iron (Revelation 19:15). He will reward those who are about the Father's business. The inheritance of the Father's kingdom comes by grace and the inheritance of the Son's kingdom comes by merited reward.[25]

THE GOSPEL OF THE KINGDOM OF GOD DEMANDS A RESPONSE

As I began teaching about the gospel of the kingdom of

God—how Christ lives in us so we too can rule over the enemy—I naively thought that everyone would be enthusiastic about this, pressing in to it like the gospel says,

> *"The law and the prophets were until John [the Baptist].*
> *Since that time the kingdom of God has been preached,*
> *and everyone is pressing into it."*
> *Luke 16:16*

My own testimony is filled with the redeeming power of the blood and broken body of Christ. Full of shame, rejection, bitterness and sickness, I am a witness to the power of the resurrection. But I soon realized that the gospel of the kingdom of God requires a decision: it can only be entered into by faith.

Just as I believe Jesus died for my sins, I must also believe He broke the curse of sin—sickness and disease—as well. I access this victory by faith, something that is much more difficult than casual, religious Christianity.

But there is a small group rising, mostly out of the next generation, who will believe God for the supernatural; they are submitting their lives to the governance of the Lord in the Holy Spirit. As we, by faith, take hold of the kingdom, sickness is healed, addictions are broken, and new jobs are created, all for persons who had formerly been held in captivity by depression, sexual abuse, pharmaceuticals, fatherless-ness, and the list goes on and on. If the Lord permits, we could fill a book with stories from just the last five years. I am convinced that the gospel was given to the down and out, broken people of this world, the ones Satan holds in his grip, and the Church that rises out of this is powerful, for she is a mighty witness to the power of God in Christ!

Had Satan known that, by killing Jesus, a doorway to heaven would open with the power of His resurrection, and His life-giving Spirit and power would fill us and so fill the world, I'm not sure he would have crucified the Christ. Paul said as much,

> *"But we speak the wisdom of God in a mystery, the hidden wisdom which God ordained before the ages for our glory, which none of the rulers of this age knew; for had they known, they would not have crucified the Lord of glory."*
> *1 Corinthians 2:7-8*

Perhaps this is why the Mystery of Christ was hidden. But Jesus did His best to explain it in the parables, 'for those who have eyes to see and ears to hear,' He said. Let us study to understand, and then rise up to take hold of our inheritance in the kingdom of Christ.

STUDY QUESTIONS

1. How do you identify yourself as a Christian? (i.e. sinner or the workmanship of God)

2. What is your testimony of Christ in you, the hope of glory?

3. If Jesus was truly an ordinary man and His power was a demonstration of the Holy Spirit in order to be obedient to the Father, how does that shift the position and possibility of man?

4. How does your mindset change by discovering the Promise to be the Holy Spirit, as opposed to eternal life in heaven?

Chapter Seven

INHERITING THE KINGDOM OF GOD

"Then the King will say to those on His right, 'Come, you who are blessed by My Father; take your inheritance, the kingdom prepared for you since the creation of the world.'"
Matthew 25:34, NIV

Jesus had a message to preach and a purpose to fulfill. Part of that purpose was to wipe out 'the handwriting of requirement that was against us' by purchasing—with His own blood—that which belonged to God, as man's Creator. We are redeemed by the blood of the Lamb. But there is more to His purpose, more which is yet to be fulfilled, even as it has already begun. This greater purpose is establishing His kingdom on earth as it is in heaven. As Jesus said He only did what He saw the Father do, He invited people along the way to do the same. Those who were willing were sent out in pairs in the power of His name.

At one point there were 70 willing participants. I call this His 'recruiting for the family business.'

About halfway through His ministry, however, He begins to experience some resistance. As Israel begins to reject the purposes for which He was sent, making instead their own demands, Jesus begins to speak in parables, and continues to do so for the remainder of His ministry. This turning point is in Matthew's account, between chapters 12 and 13. After being accused of performing His miracles under the power of Beelzebub, and then his own family wanting more of His time, Jesus begins to speak to the crowds in parables,

> All these things Jesus spoke to the multitude in parables; and without a parable He did not speak to them, that it might be fulfilled which was spoken by the prophet, saying: 'I will open My mouth in parables; **I will utter things kept secret from the foundation of the world**.'[1]

Parables are hidden truths that are reserved for the coming age, the age of the Church. Whereas Jesus had been declaring by demonstration that the 'kingdom of God was at hand,' and laying the ground work for its establishment, in Matthew 13 He begins to speak in parables about a kingdom to be inherited. These parables begin to reveal God's secret as laid out from the foundations of the world.

During His last week on earth, Jesus delivers six of His most powerful parables to two separate groups of people. Each group was given three parables each. The first group that He addressed was the religious leaders and elders, and the second group was the disciples and other followers of Jesus. The focus of all six parables is the inheritance of the kingdom of heaven. I believe that an understanding of these parables is as vital today as it was back then, perhaps even more so.

PARABLES AT THE TEMPLE

The parables delivered before the religious leaders are found in Matthew 21:28-22:14. After staying the night in Bethany, Jesus again goes into Jerusalem and immediately enters the Temple. The people present are the chief priests, Pharisees, Sadducees, and the elders. Jesus begins by telling three parables: the parable of the two sons, the wicked vinedresser, and the wedding feast.

In the first parable, of the two sons, the father owns a vineyard and asks his sons if they will work in the vineyard. The first one says he will not, but then later regrets his answer and does work in the vineyard. The second son said he would work in the vineyard, but never does. Jesus asks the audience, "Which of the sons did the will of his father?" They answered, "The first." Jesus said to them saying, "Assuredly, I say to you that tax collectors and harlots enter the kingdom of God before you."[2] The religious leaders answered correctly: the first son, because he embraced his work in the family business. Jesus connects the parable to His audience by saying because they are *not* working in the "family business," tax collectors and harlots—whom Jesus equates to the first son—will enter the kingdom of God before them—whom Jesus equates to the second son—if they even enter at all.

The next parable, the wicked vinedresser, is about killing prophets. God says He sent the prophets, yet people rejected them. The key verse in this parable is verse 43, when Jesus says, "Therefore I say to you, the kingdom of God will be taken from you and given to a nation bearing the fruits of it."[3] God is saying His kingdom will no longer be exclusively for the Jews—who were the first invited to partake of it—but it will be extended to the Gentile nation.

The third parable, of the wedding feast, is about the kingdom of heaven; it is God the Father arranging a marriage for His Son. In the parable, the king sends out invitations to all the Jewish people, but the people reject the invitations. The king then sends out his servants to the highways and instructs them to invite as many as they can, the bad and the good, referring to the Gentile world. At the time of the wedding, the hall is filled with guests.

> But when the king came in to see the guests, he saw a man there who did not have on a wedding garment. So he said to him, 'Friend, how did you come in here without a wedding garment?' And he was speechless. Then the king said to the servants, 'Bind him hand and foot, take him away, and cast him into outer darkness; there will be weeping and gnashing of teeth.'[4]

The wedding garment the king referred to was a white garment, representing the righteousness of Jesus Christ. His blood covers our nakedness and the light of His life produces works of righteousness in our lies. John tells us that if we know Jesus is righteous, then we know that everyone who practices righteousness is born of Him.[5] This "friend" is a person who was religious, yet not born of God; he never practiced the righteousness accepted by Jesus Christ the Lord

These are three parables specifically spoken to Jews. The parables are basically a judgment on the Jews, and a warning to anyone else that might have been listening. Jesus pronounces a judgment on the Jewish people in Matthew 22:14 when He says, "For many are called, but few are chosen."

This is not the doctrine of predestination, but an invitation. Let me explain by way of the old fashioned calling card; if you watch an old movie such as *Pride and Prejudice* you will hear the terminology. Today if I want to talk with you I will use the phone. In times past, before there were telephones, I would drop off a calling card to say, "I would like to speak with you, please respond if you likewise would like to speak with me." The Jewish people understood this terminology; hence Jesus could use the term "many are called." Yet only those that respond to that calling card come to the house. You get to choose how you will answer. This does not mean only a "few" people are predestined to know Jesus Christ and enter heaven; no, the whole church was predestined before the foundations of the world to be the partner and bride of His Son, and therefore inherit the kingdom of heaven. This means those that accept the invitation will enter the house.

After dealing with the religious leaders, who make snide remarks, Jesus pronounces His judgment of warning upon them, and then departs with His disciples to the Mount of Olives.

PARABLES AT THE MOUNT OF OLIVES

After relating some of the end time events to the disciples, Jesus tells three parables: that of the faithful servant and the evil servant, the parable of the wise and foolish virgins, and the parable of the talents. These three parables are directly addressed to the New Testament church and the end-time church. This is based on the key verses of the first parable, "Blessed is that servant whom his master, when he comes, will so find them doing. Assuredly, I say to you that he will make him ruler over all his goods," said the king when he returns and finds the faithful servant doing his work.[6] Jesus is the master who returns; since His return is set for the end of the church age, we know He is speaking here to the church and not to the Jewish leaders.

In the second parable, the word virgin means "bride" or "chaste church." Now, in this parable, all ten of the virgins are saved; however, only five keep their oil and lamp burning and do not tire of waiting for their groom to come. But the other five get weary, lazy, and let their oil burn out because they are no longer waiting for their groom. The bridegroom comes for them all, yet only the five who kept their lamps burning leave with the groom; Matthew 25:12 reads, "But he answered and said, 'Assuredly, I say to you, I do not know you.'" The other five beg for the bridegroom to open the door, yet he refuses.

The third parable is of the talents. It begins, "For the kingdom of heaven is like a man traveling to a far country..."[7] This represents Jesus, Who has gone away. While the man is away, there are three servants who have been given a certain amount of money. When their master returns he inquires about the money. The first servant, who was given five talents, is praised because he gained five more talents. The second servant was given two talents; he was also praised because he, too, doubled his money by gaining two more talents. The first two servants are made ruler over many things and are told to "enter into the joy of your lord."[8] Now, the servant who was given one talent hid the talent because he was afraid; the master says he could have at least deposited the money in the bank and gained interest! This last servant is cast into the outer darkness, where "there will be weeping and gnashing of teeth."[9]

If, in all three parables, the people are of the church, then why would some not be allowed to rule, or be turned away from their groom, or be cast into the outer darkness? It is evident that participating in the work of the kingdom while the bridegroom-king is away is vital in receiving the reward upon His return. Those who did not stay engaged in the kingdom's work are not permitted entry, but are put out in the shadow of the light where there is wailing and gnashing of teeth.

The phrase *outer darkness* in a Greek inter-liner Bible means "in the shadow of the light." For example, let's say you go to a sporting event and park your car in the lot; however, the lights are not lit and it is a dark night. The only light you see emanates from the oval stadium in the distance. You are in the shadow of the light, i.e., the outer darkness. This is not the same place as Hell; that is a place reserved for Satan, the fallen angels, and for the final judgment of all those who do not believe at the end of time. The outer darkness is not evil in any way, but it is not in the light, it remains on the outside for the duration of the game. The outer darkness is a place to wait out the millennial reign of Christ with His bride.

When we think of *wailing* and *gnashing* we often think of a dog attacking us; yet, in this instance it means more of an exclamatory, "What! Why didn't I know? Why didn't I do something about it?" It's not screaming and biting each other, but rather a showing of teeth while expressing the anguish of making a bad decision or neglecting a right one.

THE JUDGMENT SEAT OF CHRIST

The place where it is determined who is part of the Bride and who is not is called the judgment seat of Christ. After the church is raptured, there will be a judgment according to works.

> Now if anyone builds on this foundation [of Jesus Christ] with gold, silver, precious stones, wood, hay, straw, each one's work will become clear; for **the Day will declare it** because it will be revealed by fire; and the fire will test each one's work, of what sort it is.[10]

What day is this? It is the day of the judgment made by our Lord. "For we must all appear before the judgment seat of Christ, that each one may receive the things done in the body, according to what he has done, whether good or bad."[11]

The parables speak of one particular reward for those who are the Bride: it is called the Marriage Supper of the Lamb. This is the long-awaited union between Christ the Lord and His beloved Bride; it follows the rapture and the judgment seat of Christ, but precedes the Lord's return to rule for 1,000 years.

Will this take place at the beginning of the 70th week prophesied by Daniel, or halfway through at the start of the Tribulation? I don't know, but either will work for me.

Those who are not chosen by reason of not answering the call will go to the waiting room, called the outer darkness, which is located somewhere in heaven. Simultaneously, Christ Jesus and His Bride, who is both Jew and Gentile, return to earth at the end of the Tribulation to set up King Jesus' rule of nations from Jerusalem.

THE INHERITANCE OF THE BRIDE

"And whatever you do, do it heartily, as to the Lord and not to men, knowing that from the Lord you will receive the reward of the inheritance; for you serve the Lord Christ."
Colossians 3:23-24

Inheritance means to have a part or a place in the kingdom of Christ's rule and reign on earth for 1,000 years. Furthermore, at the end of the Millennial reign, after the battle of Armageddon, after the new earth and new heaven arrive, it is the Bride, the Holy City, that gives light to the whole earth, for there will no longer be a sun or moon. Those who are saved by grace and receive the gift of the Father will live on this new earth for eternity, but the Bride is above, giving light to the whole earth.[12] I want to give you two verses that speak of the saints who are in the *light* receiving an inheritance of the *kingdom of Christ and God*. Yes, they are the recipients of both the kingdom of God and the kingdom of Christ.

"Giving thanks to the Father who has qualified us to be partakers of the inheritance of the saints in the light. He has delivered us from the power of darkness and conveyed

us into the kingdom of the Son of His love."
Colossians 1:12-13

"For this you know, that no fornicator, unclean person, nor
covetous man, who is an idolater, has any inheritance in
the kingdom of Christ and God."
Ephesians 5:5

Picture this, if you will: a smaller kingdom inside a larger one. The larger of the two kingdoms is the kingdom of God, and the smaller one is the kingdom of Christ. This is also the Bride who comes down out of the larger kingdom of God to rule with Christ, and is the Holy City of light over the whole earth; together they make up the whole, which is the kingdom of God. At the end of His millennial reign, Christ hands His kingdom over to the Father and so it is part of the whole kingdom of God. For those readers who want to study all of this in greater detail, I suggest Dale Sides's book, *The 1,000 Year Reign of Jesus Christ on the Earth.*

"SEEING" AND "HEARING"

Once you "see" and "hear" as Jesus admonished in the parables, you can see the two inheritances elsewhere in the scriptures. Here are two other places:

"For the wages of sin is death, but the gift of God is
eternal life in Christ Jesus our Lord."
Romans 6:23

"For the Son of Man will come in the glory of His
Father with His angels, and then He will reward each
according to his works."
Matthew 16:27

The only way that 'free gift' and 'reward' can line up is if there are two inheritances—one of the Father and one of the Son. For example, in another verse,

> *"The Spirit Himself bears witness with our spirit that*
> *we are children of God, and if children, then heirs—heirs*
> *of God and joint heirs with Christ, if indeed we suffer*
> *with Him, that we may also be glorified together."*
> Romans 8:16-17

Notice the condition: "if." "*If* we suffer." This is not talking about sickness, but of labor and sacrifice in order to work and build the kingdom. Notice the *heir of God* and also the *joint heir with Christ*: two inheritances. In former times, who inherited the family business or estate? The sons.

INHERITANCE OF CHILDREN AND SONS

This is where Paul's teaching of "adoption" is helpful.

Now I say that the heir, as long as he is a child, does not differ at all from a slave, though he is master of all, but is under guardians and stewards until the time appointed by the father. Even so we, when we were children, were in bondage under the elements of the world. But when the fullness of the time had come, God sent forth His Son, born of a woman, born under the law, to redeem those who were under the law, that we might receive the **adoption as sons**. And because you are sons, God has sent forth the Spirit of His Son into your hearts, crying out, 'Abba. Father!' Therefore you are no longer a slave but a son, and if a son, then an heir of God through Christ.[13]

An elementary difference between a child and a son is that a child is one recently born with the responsibility to *love* the Father, and a son is a mature child with the responsibility to *obey* the Father. The "sprit of adoption," as Paul sometimes refers to it, is the call in us to live under the governance of the Holy Spirit: sons who are obedient to our Lord Jesus Christ. If we live as sons, then we are "heirs of God through Christ," says Paul.

The heir that remains a child is no different than a slave, and thus receives the same reward. But the child who overcomes the enemy is rewarded as a son. There is a reward for the child or slave, and a greater reward for the son who worked in the family business.

TWO INHERITANCES BRINGS CLARITY

I view the teaching of two inheritances as the answer to a long-standing debate in the church. As a young bride attending my first Bible Study in new surroundings, there arose among the women a question regarding someone who received salvation on death row: could they truly be saved? They all agreed that salvation was by grace and not works; but the real question they were asking was about fairness. Was it fair that missionaries and murderers should receive the same reward? Of course not, but two inheritances makes things fair.

Another dispute in the church is whether salvation can be lost, or is it "once saved, always saved." Again, I think the teaching of two inheritances clarifies things quite well.

Hopefully, all of this is making you ask, "How can I press into the kingdom and do the works that are rewarded in heaven?" Here are some keys that will be helpful.

KEYS TO INHERITING THE KINGDOM OF HEAVEN

Jesus, speaking to Nicodemus in the night, said, "Most assuredly, I say to you, unless one is born again, he cannot **see** the kingdom of God." And "Most assuredly, I say to you, unless one is born of water and the Spirit, he cannot **enter** the kingdom of God."[14] There is a difference between seeing and entering the kingdom; the difference is manifest by the Holy Sprit.

The number one key is to live—follow after—the Holy Spirit. The kingdom of heaven is in His hands until Christ returns, as we saw in the life of Abraham's servant Eliezer when he went to secure Rebekah as Isaac's bride. (I will address the Holy Spirit more fully in Part III.) The life of the Holy Spirit will produce a righteousness in you that is powerful. James 5:16 (KJV) says, "The prayer of a righteous man avails much." So now let us gain a better understanding of righteousness, for it collaborates with the gospel of the kingdom of God.

STUDY QUESTIONS

1. What new understanding of the first three parables has been unveiled?

2. How does the explanation of the "outer darkness" bring a new perception and urgency?

3. What, then, is the decision for the kingdom of God versus the gospel of salvation? They are two different decisions. Who do you proclaim, Christ as Lord and Savior, or Savior alone?

4. Why would Satan want to steal this truth from the church?

5. How does having two inheritances answer the question about the man on death row or the man that hung on the cross next to Christ?

6. What does it mean to press into the kingdom of heaven?

Chapter Eight

THE KINGDOM OF GOD
AND HIS RIGHTEOUSNESS

"But seek first the kingdom of God and His righteousness,
and all these things shall be added to you."
Matthew 6:33

Jesus spoke these words in His famous Sermon on the Mount. It was the only scripture I ever posted on a 3x5 card and stuck on my refrigerator. I chose it at the beginning of my marriage to remind me to put God first and not be anxious about anything. It hung there on the fridge for 15 years before I fully understood it. As I look back, I see how it became for me the "Highway of Holiness," of which Isaiah says, "whoever walks the road, although a fool, shall not go astray."[1] I chose this scripture, but then God chose me to speak to the next generation in order that He might open their eyes and renew a spiritual vision for His kingdom and His righteousness here on earth.

I want to share with you what I have learned about His

righteousness and the power of God that it produces in one's life. The 1st century Church walked in the power and wisdom of God. The fullness of Christ was seen in them. Why, then, is it not seen in us? Why do we look just like the world? "The prayer of a righteous man avails much,"[2] reads the scripture I learned as a child from the old King James Version. Believing in Jesus makes me righteous because His blood cleanses me from all sin, is what I was taught. This is true, but if all believers are righteous, then why do some live powerful lives, but most of them do not?

THE RIGHTEOUSNESS OF GOD

The answer lies in understanding that the power of the kingdom of God is rooted and grounded in His righteousness. The degree of holiness or righteousness in me correlates with the degree of power over the enemy in me. If I serve Satan, the father of lies, in any way, then I am limited in power by the amount that I serve the enemy. For example, if I follow after Christ in love, but hold bitterness in my heart, then that bitterness limits me. I do not have the Spirit's power to give love or receive love because bitterness holds back the power. If I follow after Christ in healing, but doubt in my heart that He will heal me, then I have limited His power in me to heal others or receive healing for myself. Do you see the principle? Remember, "That which God would empower He must first make holy."[3]

Before I continue, I want to clarify that when I say *righteousness* I am not talking about establishing the life of Christ in us around a set of rules or laws that dictate behavior, eating, or dress. The church already traveled down that road; it was called the Holiness Movement. What began rightly—as the Holy Spirit brought a conviction of sin through the preaching of some of that century's greatest evangelists—ended with a rigid set of rules in the following generation and the denominations that rose up during this time in history.

Like the Pharisees of Jesus' day who thought cleanliness was next to godliness, Jesus spoke correction to them saying,

> Do you not yet understand that whatever enters the mouth goes into the stomach and is eliminated? But those things which proceed out of the mouth come from the heart, and they defile a man. For out of the heart proceed evil thoughts, murders, adulteries, fornications, thefts, false witness, and blasphemies. These are the things which defile a man, but to eat with unwashed hands does not defile a man.[4]

Righteousness is a heart issue. The Spirit of God lives in the spirit of man; it is where you commune with the Holy Spirit that you have His power. When there is a disagreement between you and the Spirit of God, and you choose your thoughts and actions over His, then He will go silent and shut down, for He is first and foremost a gentleman. He will never override your sovereignty, even as He lives to execute God's sovereignty on earth. *Righteousness* is "conformity to the demands and obligations of the will of God."[5] The bottom line is this: the more God can build His righteousness in us, the more we have access to the Holy Spirit's power. If things are better understood by what they are not, then this is the best definition there is,

> *"The kingdom of God is not eating and drinking, but righteousness and peace and joy in the Holy Spirit."*
> *Romans 14:17*

THE MINISTRY OF RIGHTEOUSNESS

If it sounds like I am saying the Holy Spirit ministers His power to us according to the righteousness of God in us,

I am. Paul says there is a ministry of the Spirit, the "ministry of righteousness [that] exceeds much more in glory"[6] than that of the ministry of condemnation from not keeping the laws of God.

Here's how it works: Faith in the work of Christ on the cross legally purchased your right-standing with God, and you are now justified before God.

> *"For [God] made Him who knew no sin to be sin for us,*
> *that we might become the righteousness of God in Him."*
> *2 Corinthians 5:21*

Where before you were alienated from the life of God and walked in darkness, without understanding due to the blindness of your heart, you are now made alive in your spirit man to the things of God.[7] Spirit to spirit you now commune with God. Yet your soul remains in its unregenerate condition. Therefore, there is a work of righteousness still to be accomplished in you. How you think in your heart is how you will live; therefore, the Holy Spirit begins a ministry of righteousness in order to conform your thoughts, will, and emotions to the demands and obligations of the will of God. In other words, when you think like Christ, you will act like Christ. Remember, God promised the prophets that He would do this when He said,

> *"I will put My laws in their mind and write them on*
> *their heart; and I will be their God, and they shall be My*
> *people."*
> *Hebrews 8:10*

The laws of God were not magically deposited in your heart at conversion, but you have been given the gift of the Holy Spirit. The law-giver Himself will testify the laws or Word of God to you, and you will choose to reject it or believe it as Truth. Jesus said, "He who has My commandments and keeps them, it is he who loves Me. And he who loves Me will be loved by My Father, and I will love him and manifest Myself to him."[8] Jesus Himself is giving us a condition to meet in order for the Holy Spirit to manifest, show Himself, in us.

> *"If you abide in Me, and My words abide in you, you will ask what you desire, and it shall be done for you."*
> *John 15:7*

First, I must be "in Christ," but also His words must live in me in order for there to be such a power that whatever I pray will be done. Let me demonstrate how this works by using an experience the first disciples had with the resurrected Christ.

After Jesus' resurrection, when the disciples are in Jerusalem waiting for Jesus as He instructed them, having breathed on them the Holy Spirit so as to receive Him (remember, Jesus is now a life-giving Spirit) He says to them, "If you forgive the sins of any they are forgiven them; if you retain the sins of any they are retained."[9] What words will the Holy Spirit now cause them to remember, words that they must act upon? Here is one example the Holy Spirit could have used: "For if you forgive men their trespasses, your heavenly Father will also forgive you. But if you do not forgive men their trespasses, neither will your Father forgive your trespasses."[10] Jesus spoke this to the disciples at the beginning of His ministry, when He taught them to pray.

Think about this: The first words Jesus spoke to the disciples after His resurrection were about forgiveness. If they were going to walk before a watching world of evil, doing the things Jesus did—healing the sick, delivering the oppressed, preaching the gospel—and Jesus wanted them to be untouchable by the enemy, what would they need? Righteousness. E. W. Kenyon says righteousness is, "The ability to stand in the Father's presence without the sense of guilt or condemnation or inferiority. It means the ability to stand in the presence of Satan and his works without timidity or fear, without any sense of inferiority.

Really it means that you become superior to Satan."[11] In other words, blameless, and the devil can't touch you!

By forgiving those who crucified Christ, the disciples acted upon the word in their heart, and it empowered them over their enemy. The same as it does for us today. This is the ministry of righteousness that the Holy Spirit extends to all disciples of Christ.

It is important for you to know that the devil looks for opportunities or footholds into our lives. Where we entertain unbelief or a practice of sin, there we are unrighteous, because we suppress the truth that the Holy Spirit is speaking to us about that area of our life. God's will for you is to be powerful over the works the enemy schemes against you and your family. But there is a lie floating about that many believe, and it is a stumbling block to righteousness. It says you may partake of evil, disobey God, sin, and live.

A STUMBLING BLOCK

This stumbling block to modern Christians is called the Doctrine of Balaam; it is mentioned in Revelation 2:14 as a reference to an account of the Israelites in Numbers 22. In order for the Israelites to enter the land of Canaan they have to go through the land of Moab. The king of Moab fears the God of Israel, he does not want them moving through his land, so he hires the prophet Balaam to pronounce a curse over the Israelites. However, Balaam says he cannot curse them because God will not allow him to put a curse on what God has blessed. Balaam then shares with the Moabite king a scheme to get the Israelites to sin: invite the Israelite men to their goddess worship, where the lusts of their eyes will cause them to commit sin against God, thus bringing them under a curse by their own doing.

The idea that you can partake of evil and disobey God, yet not face any consequences, is a lie. Even in the era of grace it is still a lie. You may continue to live in the physical sense, but you will reap the consequences of your sin, and thus not live in the supernatural power of the Holy Spirit. So what does God use to produce holiness in us? Something the Bible calls *chastening*.

THE CHASTENING OF THE LORD

Chastening produces the fruit of righteousness, so that we may be partakers of His holiness.[12]

Chastening is the discipline of the Lord by way of the laws of God. These are laws He etched into the universe when He created it, such as the law of 'sowing and reaping,' which says, "Do not be deceived, God is not mocked; for whatever a man sows, that he will also reap."[13] This law was intended for blessing the farmer and the banker alike, but it also operates in the spiritual realm. If you sow dishonor to your parents, your children will dishonor you. If you sow judgment as to condemn, you bring condemnation upon yourself. If you have a bitter heart towards someone, then bitterness is what you will receive in return, only you reap from another field, not the one in which you sowed. For example, you may have judged your father, but you reap it back in your husband. I hope you get the idea.

When God uses the law to discipline and chasten you, He is not against you; He is against the sin in you. If you choose evil in your heart, God will give you over to that evil. Consider this word of Elihu to Job, "Therefore listen to me, you men of understanding: Far be it from God to do wickedness, and from the Almighty to commit iniquity [sin]. For He repays man according to his work, and makes man to find a reward according to his way."[14] Pastor Henry Wright says it like this,

Basically, if I decide to serve sin, God will let me. God allows me to follow my own heart into evil. Then, after I have had enough of the blessings of Satan (diseases, poverty, broken relationships, etc.), and I come back to the Father, then He will heal me, for I have learned righteousness the hard way.[15]

Chastening has a way of breaking our self-rule, turning us back to the Father with an open ear to listen to His voice in us and in His word, followed by our obedience. The word in us and in scripture is called 'the word of righteousness.'

THE WORD OF RIGHTEOUSNESS

"For though by this time you ought to be teachers, you need someone to teach you again the first principles of the oracles of God; and you have come to need milk and not solid food. For everyone who partakes only of milk is unskilled in the word of righteousness, for he is a babe. But solid food belongs to those who are of full age, that is, those who by reason of use have their senses exercised to discern both good and evil."
Hebrews 5:12-14

Spiritual maturity comes to those who exercise the 'word of righteousness.' Abraham is a good example of this. Paul said, "Abraham believed God, and it was accounted to him for righteousness."[16] What word from God did Abraham believe or have faith in? Be aware that it was not a written word, but a spoken word, when God said to Abraham, "I will make you a great nation; I will bless you and make your name great...and in you all the families of the earth shall be blessed."[17] Was this a 'right' word from God? Abraham had to choose to accept it by faith, or reject it. Believing the word, he departed from his father's house and walked west.

Righteousness and holiness are not states of innocence, but the results of faithfulness under testing. The very essence of testing is a capacity to choose between two courses—yours or God's. Unfortunately, there are many in the Body today that have never learned or been taught to exercise their spiritual mind, and therefore have become passive with the word of God. Because of this, their lives are marked by passivity and/or rebellion. Whether you are aware of it or not, the minute you became a Christian and took the name of Jesus, you became a soldier in the battle of the war over words.

THE WAR OVER WORDS

What you choose to believe and live out determines your righteousness before God. Is your righteousness as filthy rags, or is it a garment of white?[18] Words are that powerful. And the most powerful words in the universe are the words of Jesus that abide in you. Jesus said, "The words that I speak to you are spirit, and they are life."[19]

For instance, take the words of Jesus regarding His body and His blood,

> *"Most assuredly, I say to you, unless you eat the flesh of the Son of man and drink His blood, you have no life in you."*
> *John 6:53*

After saying this, Jesus discerned that not many had believed Him. Nor do we. As Christians today, we partake in the communion cup and the bread, and yet many are still sick. Paul said this is because we have incorrectly discerned the Lord's body.[20] Christ's body was broken for the healing of sickness and disease. How is it that we know our sins are forgiven by the shed blood of Jesus, but we do not have faith that His broken body heals us? It is because we are loosing the war over words.

T.L. Osborn wrote in *Healing the Sick*, "Sickness does not glorify the Father any more than sin does…Sickness is due to the failure of being taught about the body of Christ as we have been taught about the blood of Christ."[21] If sickness does not glorify God, then why have we listened to the father of lies, Satan, and agreed with his word that God brings sickness in order to shape our lives into the image of Christ? This is heresy, ascribing evil to God![22]

The word of God says Jesus bore our sin and sickness to deliver us from the power of Satan.[23] Our problem is we believe only half of His word. Therefore, we are saved, but sick and full of disease. It is time for the Body of Christ to wake up and start believing the Word of God unto righteousness; confess the sickness, and receive by faith the healing purchased for us 2,000 years ago. Healing for the body is just as close as is the forgiveness of sin.

I don't mean to make light of the journey of faith this will require, but consider that after the Reformation, with the new preaching and teaching of salvation by grace and not works, it still took the church another 100 years before they fully walked in the truth of this word. We are the fruit of their faith journey. Because of their faith, the word of God abides in us today and we know we are forgiven of sin. I am suggesting the church needs to embark on a similar journey of faith for healing based solely on the truth that Jesus' broken body is for our healing, just as His shed blood is for our sins. Oh, that we would dare to believe it!

Having faith in the word of God builds a righteousness in you that overcomes disease and illness. My own life is joining a cloud of witnesses that can testify to this truth. Jesus said, "The kingdom of God is in you."[24] We're not to run after every crusade and meeting to look for it. The healing, delivering power of His kingdom is inside us, the Church!

And so, since the source of power for the kingdom is the Holy Spirit, it is Him we must follow after. Let us begin Part III to see that the fellowship of the mystery is fellowship with the Holy Spirit.

STUDY QUESTIONS

1. A new understanding of the true, full kingdom of God must be followed by a seeking of the righteousness of God: why does God require holiness?

2. What does it mean to say, "righteousness is a heart issue?"

3. Why is righteousness so powerful for the kingdom of God and as a protective covering?

4. How has the law of sowing and reaping operated in your life? Where have you seen this law in action?

5. Discuss an example of the chastening of God. How did it bring righteousness?

6. Explain your reaction to "War Over Words."

PART III

THE FELLOWSHIP
OF THE MYSTERY

"And to make all see what is the fellowship of the mystery,
which from the beginning of the ages has been hidden in God
who created all things through Jesus Christ."
Ephesians 3:9

Chapter Nine

CHRIST IN US

The great mystery of God that was prophesied in the Old Testament, then preached and demonstrated by Jesus Christ in the New Testament, is now fully revealed to the Saints of God. The mystery is this: the life of God in Christ is now being established on earth, embodied in the temple of man.[1] Not in all men, but in the 'called out' ones. Together they are the *ekklesia*. Out of this world those who have chosen to answer the upward call of God in Christ Jesus[2] are now indwelt by the Holy Spirit; hence they have fellowship with God in the Spirit. The promise that God made to Abraham and His descendants is now available to all humanity, Jew and Gentile. God said, "I will put My Spirit within you and cause you to walk in My statutes,"[3] and that is exactly what God has done!

This is the genius of God: He wills to reproduce Himself in mankind and thus

establish His kingdom on earth as it is in heaven!

The great need of our time is to see the reality of God's kingdom as every bit as real as the physical world in front of us. Natural man cannot see this world, but those born from above, born of God, can see the kingdom of God.[4] The fellowship with God in the Spirit is the supernatural element of the Christian life. To live by the Spirit is to see. Without this spiritual vision all one has is religion and the traditions of men.

The cry of my heart is for the Lord to deliver His Church from empty religion and the oppressive kingdom of darkness. I minister to the broken and hurting children of God who are all saved and sick. In ministering to them, the first thing I have to do is teach them how to relate to the Spirit of the Lord Jesus Christ who reaches out to them from inside, not from some far off place. In the Church today, there is a lack of teaching about what happens to the spirit of the believer at conversion, and how the Spirit of the Lord builds His kingdom into us, which brings glory to God and fills the earth. In order for the Bride to be ready for her Bridegroom, we must overcome our ignorance and fear regarding the Holy Spirit.

The life we are called to live in Christ is not one of imitation, but of procreation. I am no more able to do the works of Christ in my own mind and strength than a fish out of water could swim. There must be in me another life, One that is capable of doing the works of the Father in heaven. That One is called the Spirit of the risen Lord. He is Christ in me. I am called to yield my life to Him, in order that He may live through me. It is the nature of how Christ lives His life through me that I want to tell you about, and, with the help of the Holy Spirit, awaken spiritual vision in you that you will never be the same. It all begins when I am born of God.

BORN OF GOD

*"But as many as received Him, to them He gave the right
to become children of God, to those who believe in His
name: who were born, not of blood, nor of the will of the
flesh, nor of the will of man, but of God."*
John 1:12-13

Born of God refers to a spiritual birth. From our mother's womb we are physically born with a spirit and a soul. God created us in this manner—in the image and likeness of Himself, Who is Spirit—so that when we 'come to faith,' our spirit man, who was dead to God, is now made alive, regenerated to newness of life by the life-giving Spirit, Jesus Christ. It is in the realm of my human spirit that I am born again of God.

"God is the Father of our spirits"[5] means He did not create our human spirit in the same way He created our bodies. It was after God created Adam's physical body that He breathed His own life into him, procreating the spirit of Adam by God's own life. The body was created, but the spirit was Fathered. Adam's subsequent 'death' was a spiritual death, a cutting off from the life of God. And so am I cut off from God—when I come into this world—until the Holy Spirit brings revelation and I 'come to faith,' or believe. At conversion, the life-giving Spirit of Jesus Christ makes my spirit alive again to God, who then inhabits my spirit with His Holy Spirit. Our fellowship with God is through the life of the Holy Spirit in union with our human spirit; Spirit to spirit, like to like.

When Jesus explained this to Nicodemus He said, "Most assuredly, I say to you, unless one is born of water and the Spirit, he cannot enter the kingdom of God. That which is born of the flesh is flesh, and that which is born of the Spirit is spirit."[6] Notice the two different spellings for 'spirit': one is capitalized and the other is not. This is because One is Holy or Divine, and the other is human.

THE NEW MAN

In the area of the human spirit there is now a new creation. "Therefore, from now on, we regard no one according to the flesh....if anyone is in Christ, he is a new creation; old things have passed away; behold, all things have become new."[7] This new creation is referred to as the *new man*.[8] The rise of the new man, the spiritual man in the believer, is directly correlated to the old, natural man falling away or being subjected to the governance of the Holy Spirit indwelling the human spirit of man. The old man, used to living by his own self-rule, is crucified along with Christ so that the new man, the spiritual man, can now live and implement the plans ordered by the will of God. Not only will the governing body of your life change, but also will the desires of your heart. In the 'newness of life' the believer must learn everything again, as if for the first time, growing up in Christ until one reaches the full measure of Christ.

Once Christ is received and we are born of God, the apostle John says we are given "the right to become children of God."[9] This means there is a difference of maturity between being 'babes' in Christ and being 'children of God.'

CHILDREN AND SONS OF GOD

The word "babe" is *nepios* in Greek; translated it means "one who is spoon-fed." Paul used it in a letter to the Corinthians, referring to them as "babes" in Christ because they were still too carnal.[10] The Greek word for 'children' is *teknon;* in translation it refers to the "adolescent, toddler-teenage years." To the Romans Paul wrote, "The Spirit Himself bears witness with our spirit that we are children of God."[11] Notice again the two spellings of *spirit*: one referring to the Holy Spirit, and the other referring to our spirit.

And yet, our growth in Christ does not stop there. Again

to the Corinthians, Paul wrote to tell them of the Father's desire, "I will be a Father to you, and you shall be My sons and daughters, says the Lord Almighty."[12] The word 'sons' in Greek is *huios* and means "fully mature, to be set with authority." Paul's desire for the Corinthians to become mature sons and daughters was so great that he compared it to the pains of a mother, saying, "My little children, for whom I labor in birth again until Christ is formed in you."[13]

From this word study we see that our growth in Christ progresses from being a 'babe' in Christ, through the teenage adolescent years, toward being a 'son' of God the Father. For added significance, 'son' in Hebrew is *ben,* meaning "a builder of the family name." Sons are born of God and mature enough to build on His name, implying that there is a familial relationship involved, not indentured service. Keep in mind that God's purpose is to establish a family of sons, not a household of servants. I tell you this so you understand that you can enter the kingdom, serve in the kingdom, and yet *not* receive a bridal inheritance. There is a tremendous difference between having a religion and having a relationship with God in the Spirit; this is why Paul instructed the church that those who remain a child are no different than a slave.

> Now I say that the heir, as long as he is a child, does not differ at all from a slave, though he is a master of all, but is under guardians and stewards until the time appointed by the father...But when the fullness of the time had come, God sent forth His Son, born of a woman, born under the law, to redeem those who were under the law, that we might receive the adoption as sons. And because you are sons, God has sent forth the Spirit of His Son into your hearts, crying out, "Abba, Father!" Therefore you are no longer a slave but a son, and if a son, then an heir of God through Christ.[14]

The Spirit of Christ bears witness with our spirit that we are children of God. And "If children, then heirs—heirs of God and joint heirs with Christ, if indeed we suffer with Him, that we may also be glorified together," wrote Paul in Romans 8:17. Again, to clarify, suffering is not sickness, but the giving of my time, money and very own life to the life of Christ in God. And by His life in you, you will start ruling and reigning over the works of Satan.

As a child of God I have the potential and opportunity to also become an heir of His kingdom. This is what it means to be given the 'right to become' children of God. As an adopted son or daughter, grafted on to the seed of promise, I have a right to an inheritance if I work (suffer to build) in the family business.

To be an heir is to have the authority of the father to work in the family business, and then to inherit it in the end. Jesus said as much to John in Revelation 21:7, "He who overcomes shall inherit all things, and I will be his God and he shall be My son."

"Sonship" speaks of rights and privileges. Sin may dwell in your members, but it is not who you are. You are a son or daughter of the living God, and you have been redeemed, empowered, and charged to rule over sin and the enemy. This is your birthright as a child of God.

The moment we come into the family of God we are in position to be Satan's master. As you partner with the Holy Spirit he establishes His thoughts and ways into the spirit of your mind; these can be used against the strongholds of the enemy.

I realize this kind of talk is foreign to many in the church today, but that is because there have been two extreme thoughts in church history that have led to an incorrect idea of who we are in Christ. One extreme came from the medieval practice of punishing the body to crucify self (i.e. flagellation), and it led us to think of ourselves as "sinners in the hands of an angry God." The other extreme is from the preaching of the modern church, which teaches that I am a "sinner saved by grace." This thinking allows me to accept myself with all my lies, thus making my sinful self my true self, without gaining victory over sin. Both teachings are erroneous because they are based on the fallacy that you and sin are one. But Paul said this,

"For He [God] made Him [Christ] who knew no sin to be sin for us, that we might become the righteousness of God in Him."
2 Corinthians 5:21

"I have been crucified with Christ; it is no longer I who live, but Christ lives in me; and the life which I now live in the flesh I live by faith in the Son of God, who loved me and gave Himself for me."
Galatians 2:20

Crucified unto His death, acknowledged by baptism, I am made alive again in my spirit—no longer 'one' with my sin—and given access to the Life of God through the Holy Spirit, access to rule over the enemy and his schemes against my life. This is my right and privilege as a child of God. As I exercise this 'right' I mature into a son of God, growing into the full measure of Christ, becoming the righteousness of God in Him. There is a righteousness I receive at conversion, and a righteousness that grows more powerful in me as the Holy Spirit transforms me into the image of Christ.

INDWELT BY THE HOLY SPIRIT

To be a son of God (by 'son' I mean both male and female) means that I live by the governance of the Holy Spirit.

The Mystery of Christ

"For as many as are led by the Spirit of God, these are
sons of God."
Romans 8:14

Dwelling inside the believer, through the Holy Spirit, is the full counsel of God. His purpose there is to take what is of Christ's and the Father's and give to the believer according to the work God wants to accomplish through them. Believers are both the Temple of God and His vessels of honor on earth. This is not arrogance, but the pleasure of God to reveal His Son in them.[15] The Holy Spirit is not a genie in a bottle granting every wish. He is the life-giving Spirit of the resurrected Christ; and as Lord, He commissions me to do the works that He did when He walked this earth.

E.W. Kenyon said in *New Creation Realities*, "The very genius of Christianity is the ability of God to build Himself into us through the Word, so that in our daily walk we live like the Master."[16] The Word the Holy Spirit speaks to us is both logos and rhema: written and spoken.

God still speaks today. Don't ever let anyone tell you differently. Everyone who is born again—even if he is still a babe—can begin to hear the voice of the Holy Spirit. Jesus said, "My sheep know my voice." If you can hear the Holy Spirit, then you can walk after Him. I would be amiss if I did not tell you that there are hindrances to hearing the voice of God, and you will be required to remove them if you want heaven's ear, but the cost is worth it! This is what the Holy Spirit's ministry of righteousness is all about. He lives in you to bring you to perfection: overcoming the work of sin and Satan in your life.

The Holy Spirit, who is the Spirit of Truth in your life, shines His light of revelation and truth into your inner man, exposing lies, various evil thoughts, and intents of the heart. By exposing them He wills to uproot them, establishing in their place the thoughts and ideas of God that are true.

As sons we are charged with exposing darkness, "for

what fellowship has righteousness with lawlessness? And what communion has light with darkness?"[17] Francis Frangipane tells us in *Holiness, Truth and the Presence of God,*

> Do not hide your darkness, expose it. Do not sympathetically make excuses for it, confess it. Hate it. Renounce it. For as long as darkness remains in darkness, it rules you. But when you bring darkness out into the light, it becomes light. When you take your secret sins and boldly come unto the throne of God's grace and confess them, He cleanses you from all unrighteousness (1 John 1:9). If you sin again, repent again. And again, until the habit of sin is broken within you.[18]

SONS OF LIGHT

For this reason, sons of God are also referred to by John as sons of light,

> *"While you have the light, believe in the light, that you may become sons of light."*
> *John 12:36*

Sons of light live a life free from the dominion of sin and its resulting sickness and oppression. Rather than cohabitate with sin, sons of light overcome it. Theirs is a life of freedom, joy, and creativity in the Lord. Because this life is based on the law of the Spirit of Life in Christ Jesus[19] it cannot be entered by adhering to rules and regulations, but by allowing His life to be formed in you by the governance of the Holy Spirit. To many this may seem too hard, but that is only what the devil would have you believe, for in truth, it is a place of power over him.

I know that, in my own life, while it might have stung a little to be told that I was holding on to bitterness because I would not forgive, when I eventually agreed with God and confessed it the devil lost his foothold in my life to wreck havoc. It was then that I knew freedom. The light of God's truth revealed sin in me so that His love could set me free.

To live in the light of God's counsel is to also live in the knowledge of God's love. The best way to explain this is to see it in Adam and Eve. Genesis 2:25 says after Adam and Eve were joined together they were both naked and not ashamed. We know God was present in the Garden. His Presence is empowering: out of darkness shines a radiant light of truth, exposing all sin and self-righteousness. His love is unconditional and unlimited. As His Beloved, we are united with Christ Jesus in the Holy Spirit. Know, therefore, that when you enter His Presence and the light of His word exposes sin, it is so His love may cover you. Naked before Him and not ashamed—this is grace. It is the light and the love of God toward those who believe. To ascend into the high places of the Father, one must fly on the wings of grace, so learn to dance to the music of His unlimited love in the power of His Presence.

> *"For it is the God who commanded light to shine out of darkness, who has shone in our hearts to give the light of the knowledge of the glory of God in the face of Jesus Christ."*
> *2 Corinthians 4:6*

> *"Giving thanks to the Father who has qualified us to be partakers of the inheritance of the saints in the light. He has delivered us from the power of darkness and conveyed us into the kingdom of the Son of His love."*
> *Colossians 1:12-13*

I believe the light of God's Presence and the love of His heart are the two most powerful forces in the universe. Together they are a consuming fire. As they burn up all the impurities in your heart and in your thought-life, out of the ash arises the beauty of the Lord. For you see, you are the hope of the Father for the glory of His Son on this earth. It pleases God to reveal His Son in you. Christ lives in you first to make you holy, then to empower you, in order that the Son may bring glory to the Father, now and forever. This is the glory of the mystery.

STUDY QUESTIONS

1. How does being "born of the Spirit" answer the cry of man's heart?

2. "Right to become" indicates an action step on our part, such as having the right to vote. One must go to the polls and cast a ballot to claim that right. How do you claim your right to become a son or daughter of the living God?

3. God's purpose in establishing a kingdom of sons as opposed to servants places greater responsibility upon His children in what way(s)?

4. No longer having the excuse of "that's just the way things are" takes away the Christian "crutch" and makes it possible to reach a perfect and blameless state by living under the law of the Spirit of life at all times. How does this truly set you free from the law of sin and death?

5. The Holy Spirit's ministry of righteousness is working to bring Christ's church, the Bride, into perfection. What is the reality of this truth?

6. If the light of God's truth were shining directly upon you, what would it reveal or expose? By acknowledging and repenting, how would you be set free?

Chapter Ten

THE HOPE OF GLORY

"The mystery which has been hidden from ages and from generations, but now has been revealed to His saints. To them God willed to make known what are the riches of the glory of this mystery among the Gentiles: which is Christ in you, the hope of glory."
Colossians 1:26-27

In the times we are now living, in preparation of Jesus' return, it is necessary that we open our eyes to see that Jesus is no longer on the cross. Having died for our sins, He was resurrected by the power of God for the glory of the Father. The Father is glorified when the life of His Son is manifested in the sons and daughters of God. Paul said that Christ in us is the hope of God's glory on earth. This was God's plan from the beginning,

"Just as He chose us in Him before the foundation of the

> *world, that we should be holy and without blame before*
> *Him in love, having predestined us to adoption as sons by*
> *Jesus Christ to Himself, according to the good pleasure of*
> *His will, to the praise of the glory of His grace, by which*
> *He made us accepted in the Beloved."*
> *Ephesians 1:4-6*

God's ultimate intention is to share Himself through a vital union with mankind, a blending of the human and the divine: God dwelling among men, in order that the whole world would see the glory of God on earth as He is in heaven.

THE FATHER OF GLORY

To this end, the God of our Lord Jesus Christ has put His hope for the manifestation of the glory of His grace in His sons of glory;[1] therefore, He is called the Father of glory.[2] When we keep Jesus on the cross, thankful for salvation but living unto ourselves, we are robbing God of His glory in His Son.

Today, the Church is being swayed by a powerful deception. As with most deceptions, they take a truth and twist it, thereby perverting the truth into a lie. The truth is that the will of God is to bring all things in heaven and on earth to unity through His Son—all things one in Christ, as Scripture proclaims,

> Having made known to us the mystery of His
> will, according to His good pleasure which He
> purposed in Himself, that in the dispensation of
> the fullness of the times He might gather together
> in one all things in Christ, both which are in
> heaven and which are on earth—in Him.[3]

Twist this into thinking God's highest ideal is a unity of

faith, and deception can be planted in the hearts and minds of Christian men. Deception leads the Church away from God's will by substituting it with something that sounds good and true but is indeed false. To think God's greatest desire is to have unity of faith—when in truth it is that His Son be glorified on earth as He is in heaven—is a deception; for they are not the same thing.

The father of lies would have you believe the glory of God's Son can be achieved by unity of faith, when in fact it cannot. The truth is being subverted with a lie. Let me explain. 'Unity of faith' seeks to draw all men together in Jesus of Nazareth; this name for Christ is the lowest common denominator, and therefore it is the widest base. If we agree that Jesus of Nazareth existed, and that he was a good man who did good things, was also a teacher and perhaps a prophet, we could unite the whole world, for even the Muslim could agree with us on this Jesus. Put Him on the cross and call Him the Savior of the world and Christians of all faiths could agree, but then we would lose the Muslim. Say He was resurrected, made alive again, and call Him Lord over heaven and earth, the coming King of this world and her nations, and we will have much division!

In His own words Jesus said, "Do you suppose that I came to give peace on earth? I tell you, not at all, but rather division."[4] Then why are we so easily deceived into thinking that a unity of faith could bring peace? Because we do not understand the meaning or purpose of God's glory. Take for example this verse about God's Son,

> *"How God anointed Jesus of Nazareth with the Holy*
> *Sprit and with power, who went about doing good and*
> *healing all who were oppressed by the devil, for God was*
> *with Him."*
> *Acts 10:38*

We will accept that God was with Jesus, but we refuse to

allow the Holy Spirit to live in us beyond His promise of life in heaven; that would mean we are no longer masters of our own destiny, but live under the governance of another Lord. This is the difference between religion as a thing of the soul and true spirituality as from the Christ within, Who alone is the hope of glory.

The fact remains that God will not compromise the integrity and the glory of His Son to rule on earth, for this was the reason He came as the Son of Man. T. Austin-Sparks, in his book *The Power of His Resurrection* wrote,

> There is something which God has which we can only have on conditions. And when we view that in the light of God's own need, 'his inheritance in the Saints' [Eph. 1:18], and of God's own purpose, and when we view it in the light of what it has cost God and His Son, it becomes a sin to be satisfied with less than all that God desires. The Lord Jesus did not suffer all that Calvary meant just to get us out of hell, just to get us saved. There is far more than that bound up in His Cross.[5]

The glory of His Son in redeemed man is the glory of God.

SONS OF GLORY

God is glorified when the life of His Son, the resurrected Christ, is manifested in the sons and daughters of God. *Manifested* means to be "clear or obvious to the eye or mind."[6] In other words, the world sees in you what it saw in Christ. When this happens in a large measure, then there will be unity of faith, but not before. The glory of Christ in the sons of God allows for the praise of God to be lifted and magnified; His Presence is made known when people are healed and made whole—delivered and protected. Man's words alone cannot do this, but only the power of God manifested through man. This is the testimony of the gospel of the kingdom of God and the power of the Holy Spirit in the Sons of glory. Jesus said,

> *"As Moses lifted up the serpent in the wilderness, even so must the Son of Man be lifted up, that whoever believes in Him should not perish but have eternal life...For God did not send His Son into the world to condemn the world, but that the world through Him might be saved."*
> *John 3:14-15, 17*

First of all, 'eternal life' is not a place but a person—the Holy Spirit of God. And second, to compare Himself to Moses' staff gives us a fuller meaning of salvation than the majority of the Church has today. Keep in mind, what happened to the Israelites, who had been affected by a plague, when they looked upon Moses' staff?[7] They were healed. *Saved* means to heal and make whole, deliver, protect, and preserve; it is the Greek word *sozo.*[8] The writers of the Bible understood salvation to have this full meaning. Unfortunately for modern Christians, they don't. Why do we not have the full meaning of salvation, and how has it been stolen from us? This is the theme of Francis McNutt's book, *The Nearly Perfect Crime.* In it he says,

> When you think about it, this near-destruction of divine healing is an extraordinary mystery, because miraculous healing—with its twin, the casting out of evil spirits—lay at the very heart of Jesus Christ's mission. For the first four hundred years of Church history Christians expected healing to take place when they prayed! How is it possible that something so central to the Gospel

almost died out?

The mystery is compounded when we discover that the enemies were not outsiders or heretics, but Christians themselves. It is as if Christians put a pinch of arsenic into their own wine day after day and then drank it.[9]

THE PROMISED GIFT IS THE HOLY SPIRIT

The Son of Man came to save (heal, protect, deliver, and make whole) the world. All who believe in Him would receive the Promise of the Father, the Holy Spirit—meaning the eternal life of God would dwell in them now and forever.[10] Before Jesus ascended to heaven He said to His disciples, "Behold, I send the Promise of My Father upon you; but tarry in the city of Jerusalem until you are endued with power from on high."[11] The resurrected Christ lives in the sons and daughters of God today for the purpose of continuing the work of Christ on earth as in heaven. This is the work that brings glory to the Father. Jesus said,

> *"Most assuredly, I say to you, he who believes in Me,*
> *the works that I do he will do also; and greater works*
> *than these he will do, because I go to My Father. And*
> *whatever you ask in My name, that I will do, that the*
> *Father may be glorified in the Son."*
> *John 14:12-13*

The Father is glorified when the life of Jesus Christ is manifested through the sons and heirs of God—not by imitating His goodness—but by the actual power of the resurrected Christ living in your belly. Sometimes this power is the grace to forgive; sometimes it is generosity way beyond your tithe; and always, it is the power to heal.

A friend of mine in our Church, Pam, was injured while on the job as a teacher. For four years she suffered from chlorine poisoning. Then she heard of the gospel of the kingdom of God and the righteousness of His word. By faith, Pam began believing that Jesus healed her when He bore the stripes on His back just as Peter said He did.[12] She began pursuing Christ, to lay hold of that which He laid hold of for her.[13] Today Pam is healed; she testifies to the power of the resurrected Christ and the rule of His kingdom over the kingdom of darkness. This is what it means to be a witness of the resurrection. Again Jesus said,

> *"But you shall receive power when the Holy Spirit has*
> *come upon you; and you shall be witnesses to Me in*
> *Jerusalem, and in all Judea and Samaria, and to the end*
> *of the earth."*
> *Acts 1:8*

Meaning, in our daily lives we are to bear witness to the power of Christ to heal, deliver, protect and make whole; this power lives in us. It is not in some far off place: you do not have to beg to get it to come down from heaven. Heaven is here, in the sons of God. He is alive and His kingdom is here! Luke 17:21 says, "The kingdom of God is within you." Paul told the Church in Rome,

> *"But if the Spirit of Him who raised Jesus from the*
> *dead dwells in you, He who raised Christ from the dead*
> *will also give life to your mortal bodies through His Spirit*
> *who dwells in you."*
> *Romans 8:11*

'Life to our mortal bodies' is a present reality. Yet the greatest enemy of Christ today is unbelieving Christians 'who have a form of godliness but deny its power.'[14] Due to their unbelief, and ascribing evil to God, they deny and rob God of His glory on earth. Let us repent and believe in the kingdom of God, for we are called to be witnesses of the resurrection, and partakers in the divine nature.

PARTAKERS OF THE DIVINE NATURE

"Grace and peace be multiplied to you in the knowledge of God and of Jesus our Lord, as His divine power has given to us all things that pertain to life and godliness, through the knowledge of Him who called us by His own glory and virtue, by which have been given to us exceedingly great and precious promises, that through these you may be partakers of the divine nature, having escaped the corruption that is in the world by lust."
2 Peter 1:2-4

The idea of the very divine nature of God living in redeemed man is amazingly true and fearfully hated by the enemy. Power of the ages to come is available for us today, if we will believe. Paul teaches us that God's own glory and excellence granted us great and precious promises in order that by them we might become partakers of the divine nature. What are these promises that make it possible for us to be partakers of God's nature? Would I not need to know what they were before I could believe in them? Yes, but you can also understand why the enemy would want to hide them from you, for in believing them, you have power over him, the devil.

Let me preface this list with Paul's words from Isaiah, "Eye has not seen, nor ear heard, nor have entered into the heart of man the things which God has prepared for those who love Him. But God has revealed them to us through His Spirit."[15] 'Has revealed' means they are and can be presently known—by faith.

We are promised forgiveness of sin; the death of the sin nature itself and its power to rule over us; the promise of an inheritance in the future Millennial reign of Christ Jesus; the promise of life forever in the new heaven and earth; healing for our bodies; deliverance from the power of Satan to hold our mind and our bodies in captivity; the breaking of all generational curses; and the restoration of all things. (I will share more about these last two in the next chapter.)

FAITH DEMONSTRATES GOD'S POWER

Believing the promises of God gives us power over the enemy because faith demonstrates God's power. To understand how this works you must first see that God is His Word. When we take Him at His Word, we take Him. This is the meditation of Hebrews 6:13-20. We are the heirs of promise, and God is determined to show more abundantly (ever increasing) to us the immutability of His counsel or His purpose. In other words, God loves to prove His Word in those who will believe.

But I must clarify: faith is more than belief. Faith is *demonstrated* belief. This is why Hebrews 11:6 says, "Without faith it is impossible to please [God]." The rest of the verse says, "For he who comes to God must believe that He is, and that He is a rewarder of those who diligently seek Him." From this we understand two things: first, God is in essence His Word; and second, He does reward those who take Him at His Word by faith.

It is not what we think in our mind, but what we live out of from our heart. I can tell you what I believe and you can argue with me, but if I testify to what I have seen and lived, then the power of God and His kingdom cannot be denied.

"The kingdom of God is not in word but in power."
1 Corinthians 4:20

When Jesus commissioned the disciples, and hence, us, He promised that He would be with us always. God Himself declared that He would never leave us nor forsake us,[16] and He hasn't, for He indwells us as the Holy Spirit. His power lives in us, and moves through us into this world in order to demonstrate to the world that His kingdom is here. The measure of His victory and glory in us will be as T. Austin-Sparks said, "the measure of faith's appropriation of the power of His resurrection."[17] Jesus Christ still lives to heal and deliver as a testimony that His kingdom is here. I have witnessed God heal legs so a girl could run again, deliver minds from the grip of depression and the pharmaceuticals that go with it, break the bondage of shame and demonic torment from sexual abuse, and so much more; I would need another book just for the stories!

The God of glory wills to have His representation on earth, and the Church is that representation. We are called to be witnesses of the power of God to overcome evil and transform lives; healing and delivering the sick and oppressed because this is the love and power of God towards us, and His good will over the works of the enemy. We have been called, commissioned, and empowered to fill the earth with the life of Jesus Christ, the heavenly Man, the fullness of God. Will you not join a small—but strong in faith—army of believers who are pressing in to lay hold of that for which Christ Jesus has laid hold of, and be His representation on earth, declaring to the principalities and powers, "The King of glory is here," and His name is Jesus Christ.

STUDY QUESTIONS

1. Can you identify where the lie of "God's highest ideal is a unity of faith" has taken root? How does it take power from the truth of Christ being glorified on this earth presently as He is glorified in heaven?

2. What is the difference between religion as a soothing of the soul and true spirituality as from Christ within us?

3. Discuss eternal life as a person, not a place, and how we can have that life now (i.e. Samaritan woman).

4. The full meaning of being "saved" is to make whole, heal, deliver, protect, and preserve. What does that mean for your life? Your family? Your job? Your community?

5. Where did the power go? How do you get the power back? This is the testimony of Jesus Christ!

6. What promises will you claim? How will they testify to the glory of Jesus Christ and to His Church?

7. What do you believe? What are you willing to put faith in to demonstrate your belief?

Chapter Eleven

THE HOUSE OF GOD

"Now, therefore, you are no longer strangers and foreigners, but fellow citizens with the saints and members of the household of God, having been built on the foundation of the apostles and prophets, Jesus Christ Himself being the chief cornerstone, in whom the whole building, being fitted together, grows into a holy temple in the Lord, in whom you also are being built together for a dwelling place of God in the Spirit."
Ephesians 2:19-22

The Church is the dwelling place of God and His witness on earth. She is the Beloved of Christ Jesus and greatly loved by the Father, the Son, and the Holy Spirit. As the Body of Christ, the Church is the collective life of the sons and daughters of the living God, indwelt by the life of Christ in the Holy Spirit. As God "put all things under His [Christ] feet, and gave Him to be head over all things to the church, which is His body, the fullness of Him who fills all in all,"[1] the house of God is the fullness of Christ on earth as in heaven. As Lord of heaven and earth, it is God's great pleasure and purpose to dwell in His spiritual house. To this end, the death of your self-ruled natural life and the impartation of the resurrected life of Christ Jesus are mandated by heaven. The gospel of the kingdom of God—before time began—is not the gospel of salvation and blessing, but the establishment of God's spiritual house on earth in and among mankind.

A DWELLING PLACE OF GOD IN THE SPIRIT

The work of building God's house on earth is not with bricks and mortar, but with the spirits of men, women, and children as they are born of God and fitted together into Christ Himself. This is a spiritual work because as God is Spirit, the house that He will inhabit must also be Spirit. The resurrected life of Christ Jesus is the link, or cornerstone, between God in heaven and God's Spirit on earth dwelling in born again mankind. In order for the life of Christ to have its fullness on earth in all realms, His Spirit needs to flow freely among the members of His body. The simplest explanation for the organic life of Christ in His people is given by Milt Rodriguez in *The Priesthood of All Believers*,

> The church is not people. The church is Christ *in* people. The part of Christ that is in you, *that* is the church! God has placed His Son in you, that Person, *that* life in you and *that* life in me is the church. When the parts come together, there is Christ. This is something that is completely spiritual and comes from the heavenly realm.[2]

The life of Christ in you and in me is referred to in Scripture as the priesthood of all believers. We are the Temple of the living God, and Jesus Christ is the High Priest. Hebrews 8:1-2 says, "We have such a High Priest, who is seated at the right hand of the throne of the Majesty in the heavens, a Minister of the sanctuary and of the true tabernacle which the Lord erected, and not man." The Holy Spirit also witnesses to us, as the Lord said, "I will put My laws into their hearts, and in their minds I will write them."[3] Through the Holy Spirit we have the heart and mind of God in Christ Jesus.

The Holy Spirit, in each believer, allows for Christ in one brother to work alongside Christ in another brother, each having the mind and heart of God in Christ, so that out of their union in Christ by the Spirit, the Presence of God is manifested. Let me illustrate this with a story.

A young woman in our fellowship, Hannah, had experienced abdominal pain since childhood. After marriage, her husband began to notice a pattern whereby anytime an opportunity would arise for an intimate dinner with him or friends, or for ministry, she would become sick in her stomach. Ironically, she also carried the gift of hospitality; so something was awry.

We asked the Holy Spirit to search her heart for the root cause; His answer was to 'look in third grade.' When the family came together for prayer, the Holy Spirit revealed that a word of agreement had been made with the following lie: "Anytime something fun happens I will miss out because I will become sick." When Hannah confessed that her agreement with this lie was contrary to God's will for her to be in perfect health, I had a vision of her lying on a cot. Without me saying a word, Hannah began describing her visits to the school nurse's office in third grade. From this I knew Jesus was with her. In tears she began sharing that whenever she was ridiculed by some of the kids in her class she would become ill, and spend the next hour or two in the nurse's office. Again, in the vision, I saw Hannah sit up and Jesus invite her to exchange her pain for His life, walking out hand in hand, turning back to see the door closed behind them and His blood on the lintel and doorposts. I did not speak this to Hannah, but as I am receiving a vision, she is also receiving the same vision; the visions are brought to each of us by the same Holy Spirit. Furthermore, as joy abounds in the Presence of the Lord, Hannah's father receives a vision of an umbilical cord connecting him to his daughter. He then shares that when he was in third grade he was regularly accosted by a bully on his way to school. To avoid the bully he began faking sickness to stay home; therefore, confirming a generational iniquity. Knowing the blood shed by Jesus from the crown of thorns heals and delivers us from all iniquity,[4] Hannah and her father confessed and received their deliverance. No longer is the joy of her gift of hospitality stolen, and she is free from pain.

I share this story, at the risk of being greatly misunderstood, in order to show you how the Holy Spirit ministers to each believer through each believer, thus manifesting the Presence of God. It is a beautiful and powerful thing to behold: Christ in us and among us. This is the priesthood of all believers, and God's purpose to dwell in the spiritual Body of His Son is the very heart of it.

> *"You also, as living stones, are being built up a spiritual house, a holy priesthood, to offer up spiritual sacrifices acceptable to God through Jesus Christ."*
> *1 Peter 2:5*

THE PRIESTHOOD OF ALL BELIEVERS

A holy priesthood is not a cloistered life, but a vibrant 24/7 way of life every day of the week. 'Christ has left the building' means the life of Christ is no longer contained within denominations or Bible colleges, and the ministry of the church is assigned to all the saints, not just the priests and pastors. We are moving away from the idea of '*going* to church' and beginning to live the idea of '*being* the church.' Since we do not go to God once a week, but rather He lives in us, He is always with us to speak a word of encouragement, truth, or healing whenever and wherever it is needed. As living stones, we bear witness to the life of Christ and worship Him as Lord—this is our spiritual sacrifice—our worship and our witness.

In these last days, there is a church emerging out of the old wineskins of denominationalism and the priest or pastor model of leadership. This can be a scary thought as one ponders questions such as "Who will protect against false teachers and prophets? Who will train and equip?" and my favorite, "Who will perform weddings, baptisms, and funerals?" I realize I just gave away the fact that I participate in this new wineskin, but I assure you it is a serious matter, for the Lord will be Lord of His Church.

This change is necessary for the Church to rise up in the power of the resurrected Christ in preparation for her Bridegroom. There is no other way, because this is the original pattern given to the first Apostles; furthermore, since there is to be a "restoration of all things" before the return of Christ,[5] it should not surprise us to see the Holy Spirit lead the Church toward her future.

Space does not permit, nor is it my intent, to write about the first century-styled church as a preferred model for today, but I suggest reading books by authors Frank Viola and Jim Rutz for this information; they are great. I want you to see something else.

There is a beauty and a power in the organic life-of-Christ-church that style alone cannot portray. Because the Church is the corporate Life of one Person, the individual saints must be 'fitted' together into Christ Himself. This is the work of the Holy Spirit, in cooperation with the saints, to bring us into the unity of one heart and one mind. When she is fitted together in Christ, the Church is beautiful in her relationships and powerful in her holiness. I must tell you, however, that while the building process is well worth the effort, it is neither easy nor cheap.

FITTING DISCIPLES TOGETHER

If you have ever witnessed the construction sight of a new house, or one under major renovation, you understand that it is messy and sometimes hazardous. This is also what true Christianity looks like in the building process. As we come into relationship with one another, working through life together, we deal with the good, the bad, and the ugly. It is not only the removal of the rubble of our broken lives, but the building up and the fitting together of our new lives in Christ. The key to understanding the building process is to know that our relationship and fellowship with one another is not based on our need to be friends, but on our need to discover truth together, and then to live out that truth together as a community.

To be a 'disciple' means to be a learner and adherent to the Truth as a Person. It is more than having right doctrine. In fact, something is very wrong in us if we only have doctrinal truths without having the Life of those truths manifested in us. It is the difference of orthodoxy versus community. Though it's good to have the right doctrinal truths, having them does not make us a spiritual house; living a life that manifests them does. T. Austin-Sparks called this our test as Christians. He wrote in *The House of God,* "The test is not whether we have accepted right doctrine: the test is whether we are functioning according to what we are, whether we are really doing the things that constitute our very existence."[6] He also wrote, "You and I exist for the life of others and if others are not receiving life through us, then there is something inconsistent in our very existence…We are the vehicle of life to the Lord's people for their deliverance from the onslaught of death."[7]   Our very existence must be a witness to the resurrected life of Christ over death. To this end the house of God is a house of healing and restoration. Healing is not God's ultimate goal—Christ manifesting His preeminence on earth is the goal—but healing and restoration allows for the life of Christ to flow through us unhindered by our wounds and the lies we believe. Because we never grow spiritually deeper than our deepest wound, the Holy Spirit picks up His instrument of choice—the Spirit of Truth—and hammers away to fit us together. Paul admonished the Galatians saying, "You who are spiritual, restore [your brother]."[8] It is the character and nature of God to heal and restore.

As the broken and hurting in the world cry out to God, He raises up spiritual mothers and fathers who are not afraid to speak truth.[9] Then, as our lives are healed and restored by the Word of truth and righteousness, that same word is established in our lives. With each member or family restored, having the same Word of righteousness in them, they will collectively have one mind and one heart regarding the Word of the Lord and His righteousness. Hence, they are in unity with the Spirit of the Lord.

FELLOWSHIP IN THE SPIRIT

When our relationships are built around the Word, the result is fellowship in the Spirit. Friendship alone cannot do this. Let me illustrate using two cell groups. In both groups the families gather together and each person shares the meaning of a particular Scripture, Isaiah 53 and the crucifixion of Christ.

In cell group #1, some members say this means healing is for today, some say it is not; both interpretations are accepted. Here the focus is on relationship to each other, not to the Spirit of Truth. The goal is for all to contribute and feel accepted for having been heard.

In cell group #2, all the saints are gathered around the same Isaiah 53, but all agree the Scriptures declare that Christ's broken body means healing is for today. They each share an experience of healing, deliverance, or restoration by the power of the broken body and shed blood.

Can you see the difference? Which group has the mind of Christ united in Spirit and truth, and which does not? Both of these groups will have fellowship, but one will have in Spirit what the other will only have in soul.

The gospel of the kingdom of God emphasizes the Word in a believer's life. It will not allow me to define Scripture by my life's experience, but instead will re-shape my life into the experience of the Word, transforming me into the image of Christ.[10]

Let us not forget the purpose for which we have been commissioned. Jesus Christ sends us into the world as a minister, a witness, having seen; we have authority to declare the works of God, "To open their eyes, in order to turn them from darkness to light, and from the power of Satan to God, that they may receive forgiveness of sin and an inheritance."[11]

POWER HOUSE

When the people of God know God as His Word, they are partakers of His divine nature, which is power and love.[12] The gospel of the kingdom of God is a message of power. Power to destroy the ruler of this world, Satan, and to establish God's kingdom. Power flows from the Spirit of God, but its conduit on earth is His Word; more specifically, the Word established in the Saints. The word of righteousness and the Spirit of Truth lived out in a community of saints is the power to heal the broken-hearted and restore shattered lives.

To illustrate, I present a story, this time about the Knowles family. What three generations of anger and alcoholism has done to ravage a family is no match for the power of God to heal, deliver, and restore. Today their home is part of a House Church network—a place to find the Spirit of the Lord and His liberty.[13]

In the first generation, Knowles men are filled with control, anger, abandonment, and alcoholism. This father is incapable of expressing love. He uses his anger to control the family and hold them down. Some of the effects his wife and their children exhibit are low self-esteem, anger, perfectionism, and alcoholism.

One son in the second generation of Knowles men said his life would be different, and he turned toward the Lord. The changes in his, and subsequently in the life of his family, have been dramatic. They now have words of prophesy over their family regarding great transformations that will undeniably be known as the hand of God upon them. They have set their eyes upon the Lord and are pursuing the restoration and place in the kingdom that God has promised. This includes the house church meeting in their home on Sunday mornings.

The Lord is at work in the third generation of this family in an even more profound way, as the oldest son continues to pursue God for a total restoration of the bloodline.

God hears the cries of the people He created in His image and likeness, but His answer is and always will be the Church. George Ladd said, "The Kingdom of God, as the redemptive activity and rule of God in Christ, created the Church and works through the Church in the world."[14] In her, God has put His wisdom and means to deliver the people of the world. God's purpose for healing and restoration is so He can then place His family at the gates of the city in business, science, medicine, and teaching—centers where His kingdom can rule over the kingdom of darkness. Having the mind of Christ, God gives them great influence in the marketplace.

In my generation, we took a job and then looked for a church nearby that would 'meet our needs.' This is not the case in the current generation of radical truth seekers. They first find the church were the Spirit of God dwells in people, move there, and then God gives the job, sometimes creating new ones, but always miraculously. But this is nothing new to them, for they have already witnessed His miraculous power to heal, deliver, and restore. They live in the Presence of God 24/7, and, as they do, their eyes are no longer turned inward on self, but outward towards the world and the needs that only God can meet. Because they know and have experienced the God Who Is, they are not afraid.

A NEW PARADIGM

The "new" paradigm this generation is living is not new, but a very old truth rediscovered. By God's grace, I would love to write a book of their stories. In their search for real answers for life's problems—search for truth that would set them free— what they discovered was not doctrine, but the Person of Jesus Christ in the Holy Spirit, the One Jesus promised would be there and would never leave them.[15] He was the power behind all the healing and miracles that Jesus did in the New Testament, and He is the power for healing and miracles today.

The secret I believe this generation is re-acquiring is the knowledge of the difference between the "gifts" of the Holy Spirit, and the Holy Spirit as the Gift. Let me clarify: while there is power in the manifesting gifts of the Holy Spirit, the "gifts" move by the sole volition of the Holy Spirit. I'm talking about being the people who, as Bill Johnson says, 'can move the wind.' They know the secret lies not in the "gifts," but in the intimate knowledge of God and His ways. It is not a power that comes from declaring the word, but knowing God as His Word. Even Paul asked whether the Spirit does miracles by hearing the word, or by hearing faith.[16] There is a difference.

It is my belief that the Church doesn't need more power. The church needs to be able to break through into the power she already has. And that power is a Person. I learned from David to cry out, "Lord, teach me Your ways that I may know You." This prayer is the secret to the power God will give the Church if she only understands its nature. David didn't ask for God's ways in order to obtain a practical solution. He asked to know God's ways in order to know Him.

Let me show you the difference using the metaphor of an old-fashioned scale that measures weight. On one side of the scale you place the over-whelming needs of the person or family you are ministering to. On the other side you place what you know of God's character, nature, will, and power to heal and deliver. Your prayers stack weight to either one side or the other. Petition for solutions, resources, the healing model, etc., draws your focus to the need side of the scale. In your wait for them to come, the devil tempts to drown you in a sea of hopelessness because you tied your hope to the solution. It makes sense that our prayers should be practical and deliberate for solutions, but we miss the heart of the Father when we do this. The better choice is to petition God for His Presence. When that side of the scale is weighed down with the knowledge of Who He is as the Redeemer,[17] the One whose hand is not so short that it cannot save,[18] the One whose undying love we can never be separated from,[19] then you have the faith that God anoints with power to break yokes of bondage. This is an unshakeable faith that looks to Him, not to His answers.

THE PRESENCE OF GOD

When His Presence is established, the strategies, the

visions, the healing and deliverance will all come. Sometimes it takes a few seconds, and sometimes it takes days, but when He is present, salvation comes. It's still a bit of a mystery to me how He comes, but I know this: He is His Word. It matters to Him what I believe about Him and demonstrate by a life lived in faith.

"But without faith it is impossible to please Him, for he who comes to God must believe that He is, and that He is a rewarder of those who diligently seek Him."
Hebrews 11:6

The God Who Is takes great pleasure in rewarding those who seek after Him. During the year of recovery that I mentioned in chapter six, there were times when Jesus presented Himself to me in a vision, in my garden. Sometimes He would walk very slowly in contemplation, with His hands folded behind His back; and other times He would set on the bench with me. This was the year He pruned me from all the 'busyness' of the Christian lifestyle. I remember asking one time, "Lord, aren't we wasting time here? Are there not more important things we could be doing?" He would just smile and shake His head and continue in His peaceful way. Then, towards the end of the year He would come and stand where the Locust tree was planted. I would motion for Him to move, but He wouldn't. I asked why, and I'll never forget His answer: "As this tree is in the center of your garden, so must I be the center of your life." Then He turned, looked at me, and said, "Come, follow me." No longer was I in charge of my daily activities. From now on He would set my schedule. I came to understand many things, but one thing I know: His great love for people. His passion is people. So much so that the God of Heaven and Earth came as the Son of Man to indwell Man in the Spirit, and this is the mystery of Christ. It is a love story and a marriage between God and His Beloved creation—Man. A story that has no end, for it was planned in the beginning to last forever and a day.

God's life in you is according to the law of the Spirit of life in Christ Jesus.[20] The beauty is in its fluidity from one believer to the next: poetry in motion. The power is in its holiness of truth and love, as God Is.

God's life in you according to the law of the Spirit of life in Christ Jesus flows like a River from the throne room of heaven, predestined to fill the whole earth; thus, the universe was created for the House of God, filling the earth with His glory.

STUDY QUESTIONS

1. Have you ever experienced or heard of the Holy Spirit working in and among His people in the church (such as in Hannah's story)?

2. How do people receive "life" through the church?

3. What would it look like to define your family's life by the Holy Spirit, God's Will and the Church? Would anything look differently?

4. What changes when you shift the focus of prayer to knowing God versus needing a solution?

5. How will you begin to establish the presence of God in your life?

6. Looking at other believers to see "Christ in them, the hope of glory" what do you see? What changed?

Chapter Twelve

RIVER OF LIFE

*"It is done. I am the Alpha and the Omega, the
Beginning and the End. I will give of the fountain
of the water of life freely to him who thirsts. He who
overcomes shall inherit all things, and I will be his God,
and he shall be My son."*
Revelation 21:6-7

It was the last day of the Feast of Tabernacles. Jerusalem
was filled to capacity with pilgrims celebrating the fall harvest
and the coming rain. All over the city, and on every rooftop,
you could see the makeshift 'tents,' smell the aroma of outdoor
cooking, and hear the joyous singing and dancing under the
stars. The anticipated event had arrived, the ceremony of the
water drawing. People were lined up along the winding streets to
watch the processional of priests carry the gold pitchers of water

from the pool of Siloam up to the Temple where trumpets—ram's horns—would announce its arrival. Accompanying the priests were liturgical flutists and singers who added to the joy and wonder of the moment.

Earlier in the week, Jesus' presence in the city had caused such a stir that He remained guarded in His actions—until this day. As the processional passed in front of Him, over the music and voices of the crowd, Jesus stood up and shouted, "If anyone thirsts, let him come to Me and drink. He who believes in Me, as the Scripture has said, out of his heart will flow rivers of living water." (John 7:37-38) Some thought He was mad with a demon,[1] but others recognized this phrase "rivers of living water." Only One other had referred to Himself as the 'fountain of living waters'—that One was God—and the people were currently celebrating His provision of water in the wilderness and today.[2]

From beginning to end, God offers us His life. From the river that watered the tree of life in the Garden of Eden,[3] to the river that waters the tree of life in the bridal city, New Jerusalem,[4] God's life flows. When John wrote about Jesus' declaration on this day of the Feast of Tabernacles he said, "But this He spoke concerning the Spirit, whom those believing in Him would receive; for the Holy Spirit was not yet given, because Jesus was not yet glorified."[5] The spiritual life of God in Christ Jesus is delivered to us and lived out in us as the Holy Spirit.

Just as Jesus offered His living water to the Samaritan woman,[6] He offers it to us. At Calvary His blood washed away our sin, but at Pentecost, fifty days later, He "poured out His Spirit on all flesh."[7] At the time of His death, the veil covering the Holy of Holies was rent in two. No longer would God dwell in a temple built with hands, but in the flesh and spirit of man. F.J. Huegel tells us, "In some measure, all believers enjoy this divine life, even those still dominated by the fallen life. For some it is a tiny rivulet almost imperceptible, for others it is as a mighty stream, rivers of living water—the degree being determined by the degree of union with Christ and dependence upon Him."[8]

God extends His invitation to all—"Everyone who thirsts, come to the waters,"[9]—but six verses later He also states the condition, "Let the wicked forsake his way, and the unrighteous man his thoughts...For as the heavens are higher than the earth, So are My ways higher than your ways, and My thoughts than your thoughts."[10] Jesus said to His disciples, "The words that I speak to you are spirit, and they are life."[11] If we want God, we must also want His thoughts and His ways—His whole counsel—for they are spirit and life to us.

RIVERS OF LIVING WATER

"Rivers of living water" are a relationship between the Word Who is Christ, and the Spirit Who is God. Together they are the living God. John wrote, "In the beginning was the Word, and the Word was with God, and the Word was God."[12] Moses wrote, "And the Spirit of God was hovering over the face of the Waters."[13] And according to the writer of Hebrews, "The Word of God is living and powerful."[14] It is alive.

The Holy Spirit is the Giver of divine revelation. But more than revelation or prophecy, He lives in us to speak—to testify—to us about God. Behind all scripture is the breath of God. That breath is the Holy Spirit. As we read, meditate, or think on scripture, the breath—or 'life' of God in the Holy Spirit—implodes upon us the character and nature of God, Who is His Word. Because the Word is alive, only those born of the Spirit are responsive to the Word of God and have eyes to see and ears to hear what the Spirit is saying to the Church. Though the Holy Spirit at various times breaks forth in us to manifest Himself in various gifts, He always speaks with the single mind of God in Christ Jesus. In other words, His purpose is to bring all things into Christ Jesus, Who is the fullness of God on earth as in heaven.

The Word Who is Christ and the voice of the Father are

brought to us by the Holy Spirit operating within the inner spirit of man. By our will we either agree or disagree with that Word. When in agreement, the living Word of the Holy Spirit—the river of life—flows through us, and our lives become part of the conversation in heaven. What God wills, he speaks to the Son, Who shares it with the Holy Spirit, Who lives it in us. According to T. Austin-Sparks, "It is the Spirit operating in relation to the glorified Man in the Throne."[15] As the Spirit is One, these conversations of the bridal chamber are shared among the Saints of God by the Holy Spirit, bringing in the fullness of Christ.

The language of heaven never contradicts God's character and nature, or His will and purpose. When He calls for judgment, there is mercy and grace. If He calls for forgiveness, the bill of debt is torn up and forgotten. Quite often the Holy Spirit speaks with God's passion, loving good and hating evil. The injustice of evil will cause the goodness of God in the believer to rise up and take a stand against oppression of all kinds, whether as a voice against the human sex trade, abortion, or the oppressive spirits of depression, suicide, and addictions. God delivers His mind to His people on matters that range from new energy sources to healing a damaged growth hormone.

The lives of God's people who live off the Word of the Holy Spirit are tall and mighty, and like Shel Silverstein's *The Giving Tree*, able to give life to others. People come to them because they recognize in them the prosperity of the Word of God, the grace and the power for living. It is through them that Christ has His fullness on earth.

TREES PLANTED BY THE RIVER

The man or woman of God in union with Christ and dependent upon Him is like a tree planted by the rivers of water.

"Blessed is the man who walks not in the counsel of the ungodly, nor stands in the path of sinners, nor sits in the seat of the scornful; but his delight is in the law of the Lord, and in His law he meditates day and night. He shall be like a tree planted by the rivers of water, that brings forth its fruit in its season, whose leaf also shall not wither; and whatever he does shall prosper."
Psalm 1:1-3

My hometown of Hays was built as a military outpost on the western plains of Kansas; it is surrounded by prairie grasses. You can see for miles. Big Creek runs along the southern edge of the city and on both sides of its banks are the oldest and tallest trees on the prairie. These trees remind me everyday of what I am supposed to be: a tree planted by the river of life.

The headwaters of the River are the Throne room in heaven; as such, the River carries forth the purposes of God through the indwelling Christ in glorified Man. Glorified Man is God's appointed and chosen vessel for pouring Himself out to the world. As Christ, Who is Truth and Light, is formed in glorified Man, the River of Life rises upon the earth. And just as the Spirit hovered over the waters of the earth in the beginning, so, too, shall the Spirit fill the earth with God by way of the River.

FROM THE RIVER TO THE ENDS OF THE EARTH

In the 25th year of the Babylonian captivity, the prophet Ezekiel was given a detailed set of designs for a Temple that has a river flowing out from under its threshold, its watermark rising higher and higher as time passes. This temple has yet to be built in the physical realm. Perhaps it never will be. Perhaps it is a spiritual temple for the living God. Here is its description in part (Remember, this is the same prophet whom the Lord said, "I will put My Spirit within you"[16]),

> Then he [who held a measuring stick, Ezekiel
> 40:3] brought me back to the door of the temple;
> and there was water, flowing from under the
> threshold of the temple toward the east, ...and
> it was a river that I could not cross; for the water
> was too deep, water in which one must swim, a
> river that could not be crossed. He said to me,
> 'Son of man, have you seen this?' Then he
> brought me and returned me to the bank of the
> river. When I returned, there, along the bank of
> the river, were very many trees on one side and
> the other. Then he said to me, 'This water flows
> toward the eastern region, goes down into the
> valley, and enters the sea. When it reaches the
> sea, its waters are healed. And it shall be that
> every living thing that moves, wherever the rivers
> go, will live...Along the bank of the river, on this
> side and that, will grow all kinds of trees used for
> food...They will bear fruit every month, because
> their water flows from the sanctuary. Their fruit
> will be for food, and their leaves for medicine.'[17]

Just as it is also recorded in Revelation 22:2, God's salvation for the world is in the River today and forever.

Furthermore, the same prophecy that identified the King of Zion as one "lowly and riding on a donkey" also gave us, "His dominion shall be from sea to sea, and from the River to the ends of the earth."[18] On the day Jesus returns to earth,

> His feet will stand on the Mount of Olives...and
> the Mount of Olives shall be split in two, from
> east to west, making a very large valley...And in
> that day it shall be that **living waters** shall flow

from Jerusalem, half of them toward the eastern sea and half of them toward the western sea; in both summer and winter it shall occur. And the Lord shall be King over all the earth. In that day it shall be—'The Lord is one, and His name one.'[19]

The fullness of Christ on earth is His Church. As Jesus Christ told John, "Behold, the tabernacle of God is with men, and He will dwell with them, and they shall be His people. God Himself will be with them and be their God."[20] This prophecy is to be accomplished by one Spirit. The Body of Christ has many members, yet is One. "For by one Spirit we were all baptized into one body, whether Jews or Greeks, whether slaves or free, and we were all made to drink of one Spirit."[21]

DRINK OF ONE SPIRIT

God made us to drink of one Spirit. Over the years, denominations have divided us with different beliefs and practices. In error we think it is our belief in God that makes us one; when in truth, it is the Holy Spirit who makes us one. While man's beliefs about God may differ, the Holy Spirit in me is the same Holy Spirit in you. If we differ in our experience of the Holy Spirit, it is due to variable amounts of water flow. Is the Holy Spirit able to move as a river through me, or only as a drippy faucet? The key is to know and understand how the river of living water moves in order that you may drink from it.

First of all, the river of life moves by way of the Cross. Out of the death and resurrection of Jesus Christ comes life. We can't get it on our own, but must receive it from God Himself. He is a great Giver, but requires the death of our self-rule in order for the fountain of His life to rise up in us.

And secondly, the river of life moves according to

the purposes of God's house, the Church. For this reason, it is important to be of the same mind as God regarding the establishment of His dwelling place on earth. A religious center that nourishes the soul can never satisfy the thirst of the spirit. We were created and called out to be a dwelling place for God in the Spirit; this is eternal life.

One of the greatest minds of the last century regarding the Holy Spirit was T. Austin-Sparks of England, who wrote,

> The river relates to the *House:* it takes its rise in the House—that is, in Christ and His Church, as one House of God. If you take anything away from that full thought—for the House of God is the *full* thought of God, it is "the fullness of him that filleth all in all" (Eph 1:23)—if you do not keep things closely related to the House of God, something serious will happen—and does happen. There are big movements, and they are not related to the House of God. You look for them after a time, and where are they?...They have disappeared, they have gone underground... It is only as everything is brought into relation to the full purpose and object of God that the Holy Spirit will go on in increasing fullness. He will stop if we put the limit of 'things' upon Him, whether the things be works or teaching...The measure of the Spirit that we know will be proportional to the measure of the purpose of God in our lives.[22]

Some of these big movements—Holiness, Pentecostal, Charismatic—tried to establish something of themselves into the Church; likewise for the various denominations that rose up out of the Reformation. While each movement of God in the Holy Spirit brings truth and light into the church, when man builds a monument to it he damns up the river to the life of God in it. When the Holy Spirit is reduced to a trickle, no longer free to move as God wills for His purposes, the Spirit of God will move on; for you see, He must be about building the House of God over the whole earth by one Spirit, without division.

Don Milam writes,

> The true Church of Christ is a masterpiece of the Spirit and a miracle of His grace, with the living Word being the life breath filling the Body. Leaders are simply meant to be midwives, assisting in the delivery and then watching over the growing Body. It is the Word and the Spirit that will bring back to us the ancient language of grace and institute a new spiritual order in the Body of Christ.[23]

I believe we are seeing the kind of Church suitable for God's habitation being established on the earth today. She is a kingdom of priests, a bride preparing for her bridegroom, with rivers of living water running throughout. A common creed does not unite her; as a brotherhood united by one Spirit, one heart and one mind, she is forever the Lord Jesus Christ's. She thinks like Him; she lives like Him. And until He returns, her work is unfinished.

Two kingdoms are in conflict: the power of evil and the kingdom of God. The Lord's Church has been given a message of authority and power—the gospel of the kingdom of God—to take to the world. With this message, the Church overcomes the rule of Satan and establishes the righteousness of God. She is not alone: her companion, the Holy Spirit, flows through her as a river to bring life out of death, demonstrating the gospel in power.

The river of life flows from the throne room of heaven according to God's eternal secret—the mystery of Christ. At the counsel of the Trinity, thousands of years ago, an eternal plan was established to put forth the image and likeness of God upon the earth. The chosen vessel, mankind, would be indwelt by the resurrected Christ, the Son of the living God, thereby manifesting the glory of God before the whole earth. His reign in heaven is now manifested on earth through His Body, the Church. For this reason you have been redeemed: that God may live in you.

People are thirsting for a supernatural reality of God. Their lives are in turmoil. The answer is "come to the waters." There is healing for your spirit, soul, and body; there is also a purpose for living that no manmade idea could ever match. Abandon all ideas of your own thoughts and ways, and learn of Him. Let the foundations of your life be built upon His righteousness—His truths—and then live them by the life of another, the Holy Spirit. Taste and see the goodness of the Lord, for in Him there is no darkness, but the light of an eternal Life. This is God's greatest pleasure, to share His life with you.

STUDY QUESTIONS

1. Describe an experience in which you sensed the river of life, the Holy Spirit, flowing in you either personally or corporately.

2. Is the Holy Spirit able to move as a river or a drippy faucet through you? What fruit identifies that river?

3. What hope is given by understanding the river of life?

4. Are you ready to share your life with that of another, taking your place as the Bride and beginning a life of the spirit, entering into eternal life?

NOTES

TITLE QUOTE

1. Francis Schaeffer, *The Great Evangelical Disaster*, vol. 4 of *The Complete Works of Francis A. Schaeffer: A Christian Worldview* (Illinois: Good News Publishers, 1982), 356.

PREFACE

1. Revelation 3:18
2. 2 Timothy 1:7-10
3. Hebrews 2:17
4. Ephesians 1:18
5. Daniel 2:44

INTRODUCTION

1. 1 Corinthians 2:4-7
2. 2 Timothy 1:9-10
3. DeVern Fromke, *Ultimate Intention* (Indiana: Sure Foundation, 1998), 58.
4. Isaiah 46:9-10
5. 1 Corinthians 2:9-10

CHAPTER ONE

1. Genesis 2:7, KJV
2. Zechariah 12:1
3. Watchman Nee, *The Normal Christian Life* (England: Kingsway Publications, Ltd., 1972), 208.
4. Ephesians 3:1-7
5. Genesis 2:9, 16-17
6. James Strong, *Strong's Concordance* (Tennessee: Thomas Nelson Publishers, 1990), #2416.
7. Ibid., #2222
8. John 1:4
9. John 6:63
10. 1 Corinthians 15:45

11. Acts 1:4
12. John 10:22
13. John 17:1-5
14. Ephesians 1:13
15. Ephesians 4:13
16. Colossians 1:19-20
17. Ephesians 5:30-32
18. John 19:34
19. Ephesians 2:6
20. Revelation 21:2; 22:2
21. Genesis 2:10
22. John 4:10
23. Revelation 22:17
24. 1 Corinthians 6:19
25. Ephesians 2:22
26. 2 Corinthians 11:3

CHAPTER TWO

1. Psalm 8:5-6; Genesis 1:28
2. Young earth creationists believe in a six, 24-hour day creation schedule that does not match up with scientific dating of the earth.
3. Genesis 1:2
4. Derek Prince's book *War in Heaven* and Chuck Missler of Koinonia House (www.khouse.org) are excellent resources.
5. Genesis 3:1
6. Genesis 2:16-17
7. Genesis 3:11
8. Genesis 4:7
9. Luke 4
10. Genesis 3:15
11. Genesis 6:1-2
12. Genesis 6:4
13. Chuck Missler, *Learn the Bible in 24 Hours* (Tennessee: Thomas Nelson, Inc., 2002), 28.
14. Genesis 6:8
15. Genesis 1:28
16. Genesis 10:9
17. Ezekiel 8:14

18. Jeremiah 7:18
19. Revelation 2:13
20. See Ralph Woodrow's *Babylon Mystery Religion.*
21. Thomas Cahill, *The Gifts of the Jews* (New York: Anchor, 1999), 43.

CHAPTER THREE

1. Genesis 12:1-3
2. Cahill
3. Missler, Koinonia House
4. Hebrews 11:8-10, 13
5. Colossians 1:13
6. 1 John 2:15
7. John 8:44
8. Philippians 3:20
9. Ephesians 2:6
10. If you refer back to the number of animals Noah took with him in the ark (Genesis 7), you will notice Noah took seven each of the clean, sacrificial animals. God knew how many Sabbaths would occur in 40 days and supplied Noah with the appropriate number of animals, as well as extra animals for the altar after the flood ceased.
11. Genesis 22:8
12. Genesis 22:9-13
13. Genesis 15:2-3
14. John 16:7
15. Genesis 24:58
16. Genesis 24:60
17. Genesis 24:53
18. Genesis 24:63-67
19. 2 Corinthians 11:2
20. John 3:29
21. Hebrews 2:10-11
22. Ephesians 1:17-18

CHAPTER FOUR

1. Exodus 5:22-23
2. Exodus 6:2-3, 5-7
3. Exodus 19:1

4. Exodus 19:4-6

5. Francis Frangipane, *Holiness, Truth, and the Presence of God* (Cedar Rapids, Iowa: Arrow Publications, 1986), 54.

6. Exodus 19:10-11

7. Exodus 19:19

8. Exodus 20:22

9. Exodus 20:19

10. Exodus 24:9-10

11. Exodus 25:1-8

12. Exodus 25:21-22

13. Exodus 33:3

14. Exodus 33:9-10; 40:34-38

15. Ezekiel 36:26-27

16. 1 Samuel 4:4; 2 Samuel 6:2

17. 2 Chronicles 5

18. Romans 8:3-4

19. Hebrews 8

20. Romans 8:2

21. 1 Corinthians 6:19

22. 1 Peter 2:9

23. Revelation 5:9-10

CHAPTER FIVE

1. John 1:29

2. Zechariah 9:9-10

3. In his time, Nebuchadnezzar was the mightiest king on the known earth; Nebuchadnezzar was a direct descendant from Nimrod. Archaeologists found Nebuchadnezzar's city down to the foundation; Saddam Hussein built his own city on this exact location and vacationed here.

4. Daniel 2:11

5. Daniel 2:20-23

6. Daniel 2:47

7. Daniel 2:27-28, 31-37, 39-45

8. Our government is almost an exact replica of the Roman Empire: the Roman government had a house of representatives and a senate. Democracy as a whole is a copy of the Roman Empire.

9. Daniel 7:25

10. Daniel 7:27

11. Chuck Missler, *Hidden Treasures* (Idaho: Koinonia House, 2002), 40-51.

12. Daniel 9:24-27

13. Nehemiah 2:5-8, 17

14. Luke 19:30-31

15. Daniel 9:24

16. Romans 9:22-26

17. Ephesians 3:4-6

18. Ephesians 2:22

19. Jeremiah 33:14-15

20. Isaiah 9:6-7

21. Romans 1:1-6

CHAPTER SIX

1. Luke 4:14

2. Luke 4:18-19

3. Isaiah 9:1-2; Matthew 4:15-16

4. Luke 4:43

5. Romans 16:25

6. George E. Ladd, *The Gospel of the Kingdom* (Michigan: Wm. B. Eerdmans Publishing Co, 1990), 64.

7. Matthew 10:34

8. Philip Jenkins, *The Next Christendom: The Coming of Global Christianity* (Oxford: University Press, 2002). Jenkins is a scholar of history and religion at Pennsylvania State.

9. John 4:34

10. Colossians 2:14-15

11. Luke 9 and 10

12. John 14:12

13. Philippians 2:5-8

14. John 16:13-14

15. Luke 17:21

16. Matthew 4:17

17. Acts 2:38

18. 2 Peter 3:7, 10

19. Revelation 19:11-12

20. Revelation 20:15

184

21. Revelation 21:27

22. Matthew 24; Revelation 19:11-15; 1 Corinthians 15:24; Revelation 20:7-15

23. Zechariah 14:4-9

24. Revelation 21:7

25. Dale Sides, *The 1,000 Year Reign of Jesus Christ on the Earth* (Virginia: Liberating Publications, Inc., 2006), 54.

CHAPTER SEVEN

1. Matthew 13:34-35, emphasis added

2. Matthew 21:31

3. Matthew 21:43

4. Matthew 22:11-13

5. 1 John 2:28-29; Revelation 3:18

6. Matthew 24:46-47

7. Matthew 25:14

8. Matthew 25:21, 23

9. Matthew 25:30

10. 1 Corinthians 3:12-13, emphasis added

11. 2 Corinthians 5:10

12. Revelation 21:10-11, 23-24

13. Galatians 4:1-7, emphasis added

14. John 3:3, 5, emphasis added

CHAPTER EIGHT

1. Isaiah 35:8

2. James 5:16, KJV

3. Frangipane, 54.

4. J.D. Douglas, *New Bible Dictionary,* 2nd ed (Leicester, England: Inter-Varsity Press, 1985), s.v. "righteousness."

5. 2 Corinthians 3:9

6. Ephesians 4:17-24

7. John 14:21

8. John 20:23

9. Matthew 6:14-15

10. E. W. Kenyon, *New Creation Realities* (USA: Kenyon's Gospel Publishing Society, Inc., 2000,) 88.

11. Hebrews 12:5-11

12. Galatians 6:7

13. Job 34:10-11

14. Pastor Henry W. Wright, speaking at *For My Life* conference, Rexford, Kansas, 21-22 July, 2005.

15. Romans 4:3

16. Genesis 12:2-3

17. Revelation 3:5, 18

18. John 6:63

19. 1 Corinthians 11:27-30

20. T. L. Osborn, *Healing the Sick* (Oklahoma: Harrison House Inc., 1991,) 177.

21. Isaiah 5:20

22. 1 Peter 2:24; 1 John 3:7-8

23. Luke 17:21

CHAPTER NINE

1. 1 Corinthians 3:16

2. Philippians 3:14

3. Ezekiel 36:27

4. John 3:3

5. Hebrews 12:9

6. John 3:5-6

7. 2 Corinthians 3:1

8. Ephesians 4:24

9. John 1:12

10. 1 Corinthians 3:1

11. Romans 8:16

12. 2 Corinthians 6:18

13. Galatians 4:19

14. Galatians 4:1-3, 5-7

15. Galatians 1:16

16. Kenyon, 79.

17. 2 Corinthians 6:14

18. Frangipane, 117.

19. Romans 8:2

CHAPTER TEN

1. Hebrews 2:10

2. Ephesians 1:17

3. Ephesians 1:9-10

4. Luke 12:51

5. T. Austin-Sparks, *The Power of His Resurrection* (Florida: SeedSowers, 2002), 96-97.

6. *The Oxford American Dictionary*, 1999, s.v. "manifest."

7. Numbers 21:4-9

8. *Strong's Concordance* #4982

9. Francis MacNutt, *The Nearly Perfect Crime* (Michigan: Chosen Books, 2005), 16.

10. Ephesians 1:13

11. Luke 24:49

12. 1 Peter 2:24

13. Philippians 3:12

14. 2 Timothy 3:5

15. 1 Corinthians 2:9-10

16. Hebrews 13:5

17. Austin-Sparks, *The Power of His Resurrection*, 96.

CHAPTER ELEVEN

1. Ephesians 1:22-23

2. Milt Rodriguez, *The Priesthood of All Believers* (Colorado: The Rebuilders, 2004), 69.

3. Hebrews 10:16

4. Isaiah 53:5-6

5. Acts 3:21

6. T. Austin-Sparks, *The House of God*, vol. 2 (Florida: SeedSowers, 1999), 57.

7. Ibid., 57-58

8. Galatians 6:1

9. *Spiritual* here means "mature sons and daughters of the living God, Who, in humility, know how to restore a brother or sister in love." See 2 Timothy 2:20-26. For further reading, I suggest *The Cry for Spiritual Fathers and Mothers* by Larry Kreider.

10. 2 Corinthians 3:18

11. Acts 26:18

12. 2 Timothy 1:7

13. 2 Corinthians 3:17

14. Ladd, 115.
15. John 14:15-18
16. Galatians 3:5
17. Isaiah 63:16
18. Isaiah 59:1; 50:2
19. Romans 8:39
20. Romans 8:2

CHAPTER TWELVE

1. John 7:20
2. Jeremiah 2:13; 17:13
3. Genesis 2:10
4. Revelation 22:2
5. John 7:39
6. John 4:14
7. Acts 2:17; Joel 2:28
8. F.J. Huegel, *Bone of His Bone* (Florida: SeedSowers, 1997), 49.
9. Isaiah 55:1
10. Isaiah 55:7, 9
11. John 6:63
12. John 1:1
13. Genesis 1:2
14. Hebrews 4:12
15. Austin-Sparks, *Rivers of Living Water* (Florida: SeedSowers, 2002), 29.
16. Ezekiel 36:27
17. Ezekiel 47:1, 5-9, 12
18. Zechariah 9:9-10
19. Zechariah 14:4, 8-9, emphasis added
20. Revelation 21:3
21. 1 Corinthians 12:13 NASB
22. Austin-Sparks, *Rivers of Living Water*, 63.
23. Don Milam, *The Ancient Language of Eden* (Pennsylvania: Destiny Image Publishers, Inc., 2003), 172.

BIBLIOGRAPHY

Unless otherwise noted, all scripture quotations are taken from the *New King James Version*. Copyright © 1979, 1980, 1982, 1988 by Thomas Nelson, Inc. Used by permission. All rights reserved.

Douglas, J.D. *New Bible Dictionary*, 2nd ed. Leicester, England: Inter-Varsity Press, 1985.

Jenkins, Philip. *The Next Christendom: The Coming of Global Christianity*. Oxford: University Press, 2003.

Missler, Chuck. *Hidden Treasures*. Idaho: Koinonia House, 2002.

Strong, James. *Strong's Concordance*. Tennessee: Thomas Nelson Publishers, 1990.

PERMISSION ACKNOWLEDGMENTS

Quotations are reprinted by permission. All rights reserved.

Austin-Sparks, T. *Rivers of Living Water*. Jacksonville, Florida: (reprinted by) SeedSowers Publishing House, 2002.

-----. *The Power of His Resurrection*. Jacksonville, Florida: SeedSowers Publishing House, 2002.

-----. *The House of God*, vol. 2. Jacksonville, Florida: SeedSowers Publishing House, 1999.

Cahill, Thomas. *The Gifts of the Jews*. New York: Anchor, 1999.

Frangipane, Francis. *Holiness, Truth, and the Presence of God*. Cedar Rapids, Iowa: Arrow Publications, Inc., 1986.

Fromke, DeVern. *Ultimate Intention.* Indiana: Sure Foundation, 1998.

Huegel, F. J. *Bone of His Bone.* Jacksonville, Florida: SeedSowers Publishing House, 1997.

Kenyon, E.W. *New Creation Realities.* Washington: Kenyon's Gospel Publishing Society, 2000.

Ladd, George Eldon. *The Gospel of the Kingdom.* Michigan: Wm. B. Eerdmans Publishing Co., 1990.

MacNutt, Francis. *The Nearly Perfect Crime.* Michigan: Chosen Books, 2005.

Milam, Don. *The Ancient Language of Eden.* Pennsylvania: Destiny Image Publishers, Inc., 2003.

Missler, Chuck. *Learn the Bible in 24 Hours.* Tennessee: Thomas Nelson, Inc., 2002.

Nee, Watchman. *The Normal Christian Life.* England: Kingsway Publications, Lottbridge Drove, Eastbourne, 1972.

Osborn, T.L. *Healing the Sick.* Tulsa: Harrison House Publishers, 1991.

Rodriguez, Milt. *The Priesthood of All Believers.* Colorado: The Rebuilders, 2004. www.therebuilders.org.

Schaeffer, Francis. *The Great Evangelical Disaster,* vol. 4 of *The Complete Works of Francis A. Schaeffer: A Christian Worldview.* Illinois: Good News Publishers, 1982.

Sides, Dale. *The 1,000 Year Reign of Jesus Christ on the Earth.* Virginia: Liberating Publications, Inc., 2006. www.liberatingpublications.com

ABOUT THE AUTHOR

Shay Meckenstock has been involved in healing and discipleship ministry for 20 years.

She is a graduate of Wagner Leadership Institute in Colorado Springs, Colorado.

She currently trains and equips lay people for home church ministry.

Shay lives in Hays, Kansas with her husband. They have three married daughters, and four grandchildren.

QUICK ORDER FORM

Web orders: Place your order online at
www.auraproductions.org

Postal orders: Send the completed Quick Order Form to
Aura Productions LLC, 106 West 17th, Hays, Kansas, 67601.

Please make checks payable to Aura Productions LLC.

The Mystery of Christ: A Radical Truth...Lived
ISBN-13   978-0-9794167-0-5
Number of copies:_____

Name: _____

Address: _____

City: _____ State: _____ Zip: _____

Telephone: _____

Email: _____

Cost per book: $12.95
Shipping: Add $5 for first book and $3 for each additional
copy.

**Attention colleges and universities, corporations, and
religious organizations:** Quality discounts are available on bulk
purchases of this book for educational and training purposes, fund-
raising, or gift-giving. Special books, workbooks, or book excerpts
can also be created to fit your specific needs. For information contact
Sales, Aura Productions LLC, 106 West 17th, Hays, Kansas, 67601
(785) 259-6962.